The

Image

Merchants

THE IMAGE MERCHANTS

THE FABULOUS WORLD OF PUBLIC RELATIONS

BY IRWIN ROSS

DOUBLEDAY & COMPANY, INC., GARDEN CITY, N.Y.

For Annette and Joe

ACKNOWLEDGMENTS   A little more than a fourth of this book first appeared, in different form, as a series of articles in the New York *Post*. I am grateful to Dorothy Schiff, publisher of the *Post*, and to James A. Wechsler, its editor, for the opportunity to write the articles and use them in this volume. My thanks, as well, to Daniel Bell, Jason Epstein, Spencer Klaw, Irving Kristol, Ken McCormick, Daniel Seligman, and Henry Volkening for their varied encouragement and assistance.

Contents

The

Image

Merchants

1

Client,

Typewriter and

Mimeograph

Machine

Do you want to sell a product, win a proxy fight, fumigate an odious reputation, project a new "corporate personality," sway a Congressional vote, publicize a worthy cause or just get your picture in the paper?

If you have any of these desires, you are obviously in the market for public relations.

Public relations is without doubt one of the most volatile and fastest-growing service trades in the United States today. It is also one of the last frontiers open to free, exuberant and often quite impecunious private enterprise. A client, a typewriter and a mimeograph machine are the meager essentials for the launching of a PR firm; the duplex office suite nestling in the clouds, complete to built-in bar and shower stall, is the not unrealistic aspiration. Some practitioners make it in a few short years. A lot more try.

Edward L. Bernays, an early missionary in the field, recalled recently, "Ivy Lee would say, 'This is an art and it will die with us.' I would say, 'This is a science that will live as long as society functions.'"

The "scientific" character of public relations is debatable, but Bernays' optimism has been more than justified. In 1935, the year after Ivy Lee died, there were but ten listings under "public relations" in the Manhattan classified directory; the 1959 enumeration covered eight columns.

In mid-1959, the Public Relations Society had approximately 3,000 members, a 50 per cent increase in four years; the American Public Relations Association, approximately 1,200. Shirley D. Smith, executive director of PRSA, estimated that there were 8,000 to 10,000 "professionals" who could qualify for membership in his group. Add the normal complement of secretaries, clerks, bookkeepers, messengers and mimeograph operators, and one gets a figure approximately the "more than 100,000" which the *Public Relations News,* the industry's weekly newsletter, estimated in 1959 as our current PR population coast to coast. These individuals include both public relations personnel on the staffs of corporations and other institutions, as well as the employees of independent PR consulting firms. A number of advertising agencies also maintain public relations departments or subsidiaries.

As with advertising, the largest concentration of public relations talent is in New York City, but in most regions of the country a reporter can no longer forage for material without finding a PR man at his elbow. This was hardly the case twenty-five years ago. Many corporations have substantial public relations departments and also employ outside firms. There are few government bureaus, charitable organizations, churches, military headquarters—and certainly no self-respecting Hollywood or Broadway personalities—which do not have at least one PR man on tap.

Labor organizations are less PR "oriented" than management, though many unions have staff press agents—who often also edit the union journal. A few unions, like the auto workers and the mine workers, run fair-sized operations (though much smaller than those in corporations). Even newspapers and magazines seem to require the services of press agents. Time, Inc. has several on its payroll; the New York *Herald Tribune* used to retain Tex McCrary.

Despite its immense popularity, there is considerable confusion as to just what public relations is. No universally accepted definition has ever emerged. PR men, whose activities frequently leave them in a state of verbal self-intoxication, favor high-flown descriptions of their function. "Public relations," writes Bernays, "is the attempt, by information, persuasion, and adjustment, to engineer public support for an activity, cause, movement or institution." From this came Bernays' famous shorthand definition of PR as "the engineering of consent"—a phrase whose manipulative ring (which Bernays did not intend) in itself constituted a grievous PR blunder.

To John W. Hill, public relations is simply "the management function which gives the same organized and careful attention to the asset of good will as is given to any other major asset of the business."

Herbert M. Baus is more ambitious: "Public relations is a combination of philosophy, sociology, economics, language, psychology, journalism, communication, and other knowledges into a system of human understanding."

Charles Plackard, on the other hand, thinks of public relations as "merely human decency which flows from a good heart."

Fortune, with commendable brevity, calls it "good perform-ance, publicly appreciated because adequately communicated."

The difficulty with all these definitions is that they as fre-quently describe an aspiration as a reality—and an aspiration which always relegates mere publicity to a distinctly subordinate role.

In truth, "public relations" is a capacious term, covering a multitude of activities. At one extreme is pure consulting work, in which the PR counsel advises the board of directors on the company's "posture" toward the public—without turning his hand to a lowly press release. Most prestige attaches to this function, which at its ideal involves influencing basic institu-tional practices with a view to creating the most favorable impact on public opinion. All sorts of advice may be proffered—on the timing of a price increase, the location of a new plant, the type of TV show to be sponsored, the establishment of a foundation, the dexterous way of avoiding an appearance before a Congres-sional committee—or what the president should say if an appear-ance cannot be avoided.

This is the upper stratosphere of public relations; few prac-titioners breathe its rarefied air for much of their working day. At the opposite extreme are the uninhibited efforts of the press agents, who devote themselves to securing as much free space as they can wangle out of indulgent editors; their success is measured by volume of "client mention." A variation of press agentry is "product publicity"—which is nothing less than free advertising for consumer products in the news columns or over the air waves, often secured through the most ingenious means.

The PR man may have other functions, as well. He may over-see a company's institutional advertising, do a bit of lobbying, plot marketing studies, advise on labor relations. To the provincial client he may open the doors to the glittering worlds of New York or Washington. A few independent consultants are accomplished all-around confidants and hand-holders, advising their clients—much as a family lawyer would, and often with the same lack of competence—on everything from their investments to the psychotherapy of their children. Among the fraternity, it is generally felt that the more deeply a PR counsel can get himself entwined in the affairs of his client, the surer he is of retaining the account.

Terminology, however, remains a sensitive point. There is assuredly a reasonable distinction between formulating the strategy of public relations on the highest corporate levels and the sheer pursuit of publicity. But most PR men do a good deal of workaday publicity, yet hate to be known as "press agents"; the term "public relations counsel" is preferred for its air of professional distinction. Practitioners of more modest pretension compromise on "publicist"—which not so long ago meant a writer "on matters of public policy." Only in the entertainment world will a press agent so characterize himself; in editorial offices, of course, all PR people are known as press agents.

In fact, and without much distortion, the whole breed may be called the Image Merchants—the men who endlessly "create," "delineate," "adumbrate" and "project" the most flattering available "images" of their clients. "Image" is perhaps the favorite noun in public relations; "project" the most popular verb; their conjunction the most shopworn phrase in the business. Yet image-projection epitomizes the current practice of PR—whether the image be that of a corporation, an industry, a product, a trade union, an ecdysiast or an opera star. In every case, the job of the PR man is the same—the pursuit of public approval through the merchandising of favorable impressions of his client. The techniques vary enormously, of course.

Some are direct, others imaginatively indirect. Planting a band leader's name in a Broadway column, attached to an appropriate (and generally unuttered) witticism, or undraping a starlet's torso across four columns of newsprint, represents a frontal assault on an indulgent public. The means (in the old days it was called "space-grabbing") are straightforward, and the desired image somewhat lacking in subtlety. At a further remove is the publicity man who will push the sale of hats by getting them worn by society women in all the best restaurants in town—thereby "breaking" the society pages with pictures of his client's product.

Considerably more indirect is the operation of a PR firm which will prosecute a client's proxy fight by planting false rumors about the opposition, or a corporation which will spruce up a tarnished reputation by subsidizing medical research or touring a symphony orchestra, or a truck manufacturer which will seek to overcome the baleful PR effects of a long strike by launching a nationwide campaign in behalf of better roads. The latter two instances involve not mere publicity mongering but the dexterous creation of what are called "situations of reality"—another favorite PR phrase—which will presumably call forth a favorable response from the public.

Although their services are in wide demand, PR men often feel distinctly unappreciated. Not by businessmen, by and large, who once converted to the PR gospel often regard their counsels as wondrous guardians of some arcane science. And not by the young, who tend to consider public relations as one of the "glamour" professions—like television, advertising, or the newspaper business. "I keep getting these youngsters straight out of college," says Milton Fairman, PR chief of the Borden Company, "who seem to think that we spend all our time taking people to expensive lunches and indulging in all sorts of agreeable skulduggery."

PR's critics are largely found among journalists and academicians, but they also include congressmen appalled at the public relations efforts of the executive branch, labor leaders jealous of the PR budgets of industry, and occasional businessmen who feel betrayed by some fast-talking PR type. Journalists tend to be suspicious both of the deft indirection of the sophisticated public relations man and the crude importuning of the old-fashioned press agent. The former they regard as "manipulative" in some ill-defined way and the latter as a downright annoyance. The general disdain for the breed exists in all editorial shops, despite the fact that most journalists admire the proficiency—and even the integrity—of individual practitioners.

This jaundiced appraisal explains much of the sensitivity of the average PR man. He feels that his work is often misunderstood by the press, that many of his activities are manipulative, if at all, only in an innocuous sense, and that every kind of newsgathering organization depends on his services to a far greater extent than it cares to acknowledge. There is a measure of truth in these assertions, but they are marvelously unpersuasive to editorial workmen. The PR man is thus forced to try to raise his status through his own unaided efforts—by such devices as upgrading himself from "press agent" to "PR counsel" and talking solemnly, and generally unspecifically, about the ethical considerations of the "profession." His motive in these exertions, of course, is only partly to raise his self-esteem vis-à-vis the journalist; he also wants to impress clients.

The truth, of course, is that both the detractors and defenders have a case. There are widely contrasting styles among PR practitioners. Some play it clean and some play it dirty. A few examples may help to elucidate the point. The nature of the unflattering material is such—both here and elsewhere in this volume—that some of these instances have to be rendered anonymously; in certain cases, anonymity was a condition imposed by the source. But all these stories are true; any student of public relations can check them against his own impressions. On the other hand, the reader is urged not to draw any sweeping conclusions from these passages. Improprieties occur in PR as in any other field, but a great many practitioners operate ethically and are as dismayed as any outsider at the unappetizing exploits of their less responsible brethren.

Suppose the PR assignment is to build up grass-roots support for or against a piece of legislation. One can recruit community leaders to the cause, issue press releases, publish ads, appeal to the public through speeches, radio and television. Such was the design, for example, for the massive nationwide campaign which Hill and Knowlton, Inc. launched in 1954 on behalf of the producers of natural gas. The goal was to liberate their clients from the burden of federal price control, and the method was a remorseless gusher of propaganda, inundating every medium and costing in excess of $1,600,000 over a seventeen-month period. Hill and Knowlton's arguments could be attacked, not its ethics.

An additional method, in which the Carl Byoir organization is adept, is to hoodwink the yokels. In its fight a few years ago against the truckers, Byoir & Associates, representing the railroads, showed great ingenuity in disguising the source of its propaganda. Instead of merely having the railroads speak for themselves, Byoir specialized in "fronts"—existing groups which could be infiltrated and turned into mouthpieces for the railroads, or dummy organizations especially created for the purpose.

All in all, it was a dazzling performance in the creation and nurture of false façades—in its virtuosity perhaps equaled only by the Communists during the heyday of the Popular Front. And the Byoir maneuver was far more successful: in the end the governor of Pennsylvania vetoed the legislation (raising the weight limits of trucks on the roads) which the truckers wanted and the railroads opposed.

The care and feeding of the press is a standard part of PR practice. No one objects to the free lunch or cocktail party, but on occasion hospitality is carried to extreme forms.

A new employee in the PR department of a large corporation was called in one afternoon. "Tom, this is a bit embarrassing," his boss said, "but there's no one else around to handle the assignment."

The "assignment" was to take care of a reporter on a spree in a near-by pub.

"He always calls us when he's drunk and out of pocket," the boss said. "He's kind of on our payroll."

Following instructions, Tom picked up the reporter, paid his check, took him on a round of two or three other bars. By 10:00 P.M. Tom wanted to go home and so he cut short the festivities. "Who's your doll?" he asked. It was the hat-check girl, and she cost thirty dollars. Tom slid the money across the table and took his leave. This was the standard evening's ritual, the boss had said. It paid off in a decent news break once or twice a month.

It is not only the press or public which may be victimized by high-powered PR men. At times clients are duped. One deft operator used to make it a practice, whenever possible, to secure copies of *Time* and *Newsweek* a day or two before they appeared on the newsstands. If he discovered a story about a prospective client—for which he was in no way responsible—he would immediately telephone the gentleman concerned and urge him to buy next week's issue.

"I may be wrong," he would suggest cautiously, "but I think I've managed to plant something on your operation." He was not wrong, of course, and the prospect was likely to be greatly impressed.

A variant on this maneuver, practiced by one PR man, is to secure an advance manuscript or proof copy of an article about to appear on a client. This may be a difficult matter, requiring co-operative friends in the editorial office—or in the typing room. The PR man then inserts several paragraphs highly damaging to his client, has the manuscript retyped, and sends it to the subject. Outcries of dismay, but the PR counsel is reassuring.

"I'll work on the writer," he says. "With any luck, I'll get him to take out that rot. But it may cost a little money."

The article finally appears, bereft of the unflattering material which it never contained, and the client regards the PR man as a genius. He does not mind paying an additional three thousand dollars or so for "expenses."

As suggested earlier, by no means do all or even a majority of practitioners attempt such sleight of hand. At its best, public relations performs several useful functions—chief among them, perhaps, being its role in lubricating the channels of communication. A publicity man who gets a reticent client to talk often does him a service and also eases the task of the harassed reporter. Nor can anyone object to a PR counsel who coaches a client on how to put his best foot forward. Moreover, a lot of worth-while things do get done whose original impulse was the all too human desire on the client's part to achieve his brief glow in the headlines. Corporate policy on occasion does get shifted—even in such matters as recognizing a union or hiring Negroes—because it will allow the firm to present a more agreeable face to the public.

And often the coups carried off by PR men are quite harmless. The new client is a playboy. Yet he comes from an old-line family and at age forty has sudden pretensions to sobriety. How transform him into a man of distinction? Assets: plenty of money, a couple of directorships, a good speaking voice. The PR tactic, obviously, is to get him on his feet before civic groups and start the mimeographs cranking. But something is lacking—a tag line, an easily identifiable relationship with some serious pursuit. The PR counsel, who is well connected, approaches the National Society of Industrial Mediators (which is not its name). Wouldn't it be possible to elect his client to some office? Indeed, it would be, and the PR man gets the distinct impression that a generous donation would speed the election.

The client writes a check for ten thousand dollars and in due course is elected president. Thereafter, when the press releases go out, he is dubbed president of the NSIM, and it becomes easy to get him speaking invitations around the country. A new image gradually takes shape.

Much PR work is unabashed selling. Bill Kaduson, an old United Press hand who now works for Edward Gottlieb & Associates, Ltd., has for some years been trying to persuade the American people of the virtues of cognac. The technique, simply put, is to try to get cognac and its uses mentioned in every possible context (including this one). It is a standard program of product publicity, relieved every so often by a stunt.

In 1957, on the occasion of President Eisenhower's sixty-seventh birthday, Kaduson procured from his client several bottles of cognac distilled sixty-seven years before. It was to be a birthday gift for the President, but Kaduson did not try to get White House co-operation for the presentation; he might well have been turned down. Instead he insured the precious bottles for ten thousand dollars, loaded them into the back of his car and headed for Washington. Early in the morning, beret clapped to his skull, he showed up in the city room of the Washington *Daily News*, got his picture taken as he ceremoniously poured the contents of the bottles into a small keg especially designed for the presentation.

Then he gave the precious cargo to two uniformed guards, whom he had hired for the occasion, and they conveyed it to the White House. When the secret-service men accepted the gift, Kaduson had scored. Headlines sprouted around the country, all mentioning cognac and Ike. This also is part of public relations.

In its own behalf, the PR fraternity argues that it does more than promote communication, build up personalities, sell products, advocate a client's case before the bar of public opinion— and bestow a few blessings on the community as by-products of its efforts to shore up institutional façades. PR men become quite impassioned in suggesting that "ethical public relations" involves harmonizing the client's interests with the public interest. John W. Hill, for example, writes that "The foundation for good public relations consists of sound policies and good works conceived in the public interest."

Ben Sonnenberg is persuaded that "A business or other undertaking . . . cannot, except for a brief time, throw a veil of glamour around policies or products that are inherently shoddy and antisocial. The enterprise which would gain public favor must first be rooted in sound, constructive achievement or purpose."

And Paul Garrett, the man who established General Motors' public relations department in 1931, has gone so far as to state that "Public relations is . . . a philosophy of management—which deliberately and with enlightened selfishness places the broad interest of the customer first in every decision affecting the operation of the business"—a statement which, if true, would seem to give GM's stockholders considerable grounds for complaint.

These declarations contain a core of truth, of course. To gain widespread acceptance over a period of time, a corporation's policies must *seem* to be in the public interest. Whether they are or not is often a matter of considerable debate. PR's theoreticians, however, speak as if the "public interest" were some objectively verifiable substance, which has only to be discovered to be spun into a fine raiment of virtue covering their naked clients. The sad fact, of course, is that no party to a controversy lacks the imagination to identify its own private interest with the public interest.

Public interest is so elastic a concept that even the unaided client can stretch it to cover a multitude of private preferences —short of trading with the enemy in time of war. Of course, certain other corporate policies, which were once widespread, are now generally regarded as antisocial—such as a refusal to bargain collectively, hiring thugs to beat up strikers, discriminating in employment against Catholics or Jews or (in the North) Negroes, or indulging in blatantly misleading advertising. Other policies are unarguably in the public interest—contributing to the local Community Chest, avoiding stream pollution, or sponsoring a first-rate series of television documentaries. The PR man who can persuade a client to embrace these good works has bought a claim to rectitude which he can vigorously exploit.

Much of PR's efforts, however, directly enter the realm of controversy—where the concept of public interest is hardly a guide to corporate policy but rather a rhetorical device to win acceptance for policies which might otherwise be unpalatable. Hill and Knowlton, according to their lights, were acting in the public interest when defending the natural gas producers against the incubus of federal price regulation. Equally vocal for the public interest were their opponents, who feared that the consumer of gas would be burdened with unfair charges if the producers were given their head.

Who speaks for the public interest in a labor dispute—the employer who decries the inflationary impact of wage increases, or the union which insists that the employer is using the excuse of wage increases to impose unconscionable price increases? Who spoke for the public interest in the tidelands oil dispute or in the controversy over Dixon-Yates? What is clear is that, in an atmosphere drenched with the clichés of public relations, few people any longer speak up in the name of an avowedly private interest.

An examination of the range of public relations activities in this country is also likely to show that while the shibboleth is public interest, the real goal is public acceptance of the status quo in our economic arrangements. What PR is trying to sell, in an ultimate sense, are the merits of a particular corporation and the merits of the American capitalist system.

This statement is obviously subject to certain qualifications. Much of what is normally included under the rubric of public relations—such as fund-raising, product publicity, entertainment press agentry—has nothing to do with institutional validation. It is also true that the same techniques used by business PR are available—and are used, though not to the same degree—by labor

unions, nonprofit organizations, churches, government and the
military. The techniques of PR are in themselves neutral. But
the biggest budgets, the highest priced and usually the most expert talent are maintained by industry.

In 1955, *Fortune* estimated that nearly 5,000 corporations
either had their own PR departments, retained outside counsel,
or did both. (Since then, the figure is likely to have increased;
PR has never shown a downward trend.) At the beginning of
1959, according to the calculations of the *Public Relations News*,
there were approximately 1,250 PR companies in the country.
Business firms made up the great majority of their clients. Labor's involvement in public relations is by comparison small. It
is a rare union which will employ an outside counsel, and, as
mentioned earlier, the PR staffs of international unions are
undernourished compared with industry.

The goal is not merely to sell American capitalism—which is
hardly a controversial matter any more (whatever did happen
to the Socialist party?). Rather, it is to sell American capitalism
as presently constituted—with certain useful improvements, such
as lower taxes and more tractable unions. The far-flung public
relations staffs of General Motors or U. S. Steel are hardly interested in reforming our economy along lines sketched by J. K.
Galbraith or Leon Keyserling. Only an occasional maverick
businessman promotes himself as a latter-day New Dealer.

"The challenge that faces us," Paul Garrett said in 1938, "is to
shake off our lethargy and through public relations make the
American plan of industry stick. For, unless the contributions of
the system are explained to consumers in terms of their own interest, the system itself will not stand against the storm of falla-
cies that rides the air . . ."

It was precisely that challenge which inspired the birth of

public relations, as an organized discipline, shortly after the turn of the century. Ironically, public relations owes both its establishment and vast expansion to two great surges of social reform —the era of the muckrakers and the era of the New Deal. PR was the businessman's answer to his detractors.

The origins of public relations can of course be traced further back. Admiring historians even manage to uncover its antecedents in antiquity. Cutlipp and Center, in their textbook *Effective Public Relations,* remind their students that "Legend has it that Demosthenes had his own publicity agent." Bernays (in *Public Relations*) informs us that "In ancient Egypt, priests were experts in public opinion and persuasion." It is also his view that "The three main elements of public relations are practically as old as society: informing people, persuading people, or integrating people with people." On this basis, of course, it is possible to make PR men out of kings and courtiers, revolutionists and pamphleteers down through the centuries.

With somewhat greater justification, Samuel Adams has been characterized as the "press agent" of the American revolution. The Boston tea party was a "staged event," designed to arouse public interest in an issue. Amos Kendall, a leading member of Jackson's Kitchen Cabinet, is described by Cutlipp and Center as "another unsung pioneer in the practice of public relations." He advised his chief on high policy, took soundings of public opinion, ghosted speeches and state papers, distributed what we would today call press releases.

As the nineteenth century progressed, politicians, preachers, utopian missionaries, abolitionists, agitators of every sort tried to influence and manipulate public opinion. Lincoln, it need hardly be suggested, had a firm grasp of the techniques of public persuasion. But public relations, as a specialized calling with a well-articulated set of techniques and an elaborate tracery of theory, nowhere existed.

In the 1880's, it is true, the Erie and Pennsylvania railroads had press agents who tried to butter up reporters by distributing free passes. The Westinghouse Electric Company hired its first publicity man in 1889. A little later, the American Telephone and Telegraph Company set up a "literary bureau" in Boston, as did the Mutual Life Insurance Company. The Standard Oil Company paid newspapers to print advertising matter disguised as news stories or editorials. Companies frequently received "free puffs" in the news columns when they bought advertising. The term "press agent" itself originated in the circus, and the calling was well developed throughout show business by the 1880's.

The business community as a whole, however, was oblivious to the need of organizing its public relations and usually downright hostile to press inquiries. In extreme form, the businessman's attitude was typified by the candid exclamation of William Vanderbilt, head of New York Central: "The public be damned."

Such hauteur was no longer possible after Ida Tarbell, Lincoln Steffens, Upton Sinclair and their colleagues turned their impassioned energies to a dissection of the derelictions, real and imagined, of American business. The refusal of industrialists to dignify their critics by rebuttal only added to the effectiveness of the attack.

When a coal-mine strike occurred in 1902, the union, because of the shrewd leadership of John Mitchell, got an excellent press, but the most memorable statement that came from the employers was uttered by George F. Baer, who pointed out that the workingmen would be protected "not by the labor agitators but by the Christian men whom God in His infinite wisdom has given control of the property interests of the country." Baer and his friends were quite unprepared for the hoots of derision that resulted. But in 1906, when another strike was looming, the coal owners had learned their lesson and prudently retained Ivy Lee as their press representative.

The opening of Ivy Lee's first publicity office, in 1904, was an historic moment in the launching of corporate public relations—though Lee did not use the term. Lee became known as the "father" of the new calling because of the prestige of his clients, his well-publicized efforts to convert businessmen to the new creed, and the notoriety brought him by some of his escapades. But even in his early years he was by no means the only missionary from business to the public. In 1905, a Boston publicity firm was retained by the railroads and soon established branch press offices in Washington, Chicago, Topeka, St. Louis and New York. The beginnings of A. T. and T.'s elaborate public relations efforts date from 1907, when Theodore Vail became president. There were other early practitioners as well. Authorities place the first use of the term "public relations," in its modern sense, in either 1906 or 1908.

Lee's contribution was initially most memorable, however. He was well equipped for the task. A Georgia lad, educated in Princeton, he had served for several years on New York newspapers and he shared the newspaperman's dismay at corporation officials who did not deign to meet the press. On the other hand, Lee had an unabashed admiration for the captains of industry and a zealous conviction that if they would but tell their side of the story, the fogs of public suspicion would roll away.

Two years after he opened his office, Lee issued his manifesto in the form of a "Declaration of Principles" sent to editors: "This is not a secret press bureau. All our work is done in the open. We aim to supply news. This is not an advertising agency; if you think any of our matter ought properly to go to your business office, do not use it. Our matter is accurate . . ."

He issued his "Principles" some months before the Pennsylvania Railroad retained him in 1906. He soon had an opportunity to demonstrate his methods in dramatic fashion. As Eric F. Goldman tells the story in his illuminating little volume, *Two-way Street:*

". . . an accident occurred along the main line, at Gap, Pennsylvania. Automatically the customary machinery of news suppression was thrown into gear, and just as quickly Lee reversed it. Reporters were invited to travel to the scene at the expense of the railroad; facilities were promptly set up for the gathering of facts and the taking of photographs; facts which reporters had not thought to ask about were offered . . . when the commotion settled down, the Pennsylvania found itself basking in one of the few good presses it had enjoyed since the turn-of-the-century."

Lee's success with the Pennsylvania Railroad brought him John D. Rockefeller, Jr., as a client in 1914. The Rockefellers were currently suffering a spasm of very bad publicity as a result of the mass shooting of workers on strike at the Colorado Fuel and Iron Company—an incident which has gone down in history as the "Ludlow Massacre." Lee set to work reshaping the public image of the Rockefeller family, an enterprise in which his "art" was notably successful. But he did not, as legend held, persuade Rockefeller, Sr., to distribute dimes; it was the old man's own idea.

By 1916 Lee had come to the view that decent publicity was not merely a matter of the corporation speaking up in its own behalf and letting the reporters ask questions. "Publicity in its ultimate sense," he wrote, "means the actual relationship of a company to the people, and that relationship involves far more than *saying*—it involves *doing*." He thereby wrote an elementary definition of public relations, in its ideal form.

Lee's pioneering efforts brought him a fortune. They also elicited a fair amount of criticism. His first job for the Rockefellers (at a thousand dollars a month) had been disseminating "the facts" about the bloody Colorado coal strike of 1913–14. As he later informed the Commission on Industrial Relations, Lee had proposed that the coal operators practice "absolute frankness." The commission, not overly impressed, interrogated him about certain misinformation—highly damaging to the strikers—which appeared in a widely distributed communiqué that Lee wrote. Lee conceded his error, but explained to the commission that he just issued what "facts" his client handed him, without attempting any independent verification.

One commissioner thereupon suggested, "Your mission was that of the average publicity agent, was it not, to give the truth as the man you were serving saw it?"

"That would represent a characterization on your part," Lee replied primly. It represents a problem, however, which still plagues PR men.

Lee was more sharply attacked in 1934, when it was revealed that he was in the employ of the German Dye Trust at a fee of twenty-five thousand dollars a year. Testifying before a committee of the House of Representatives, he made the point that he had no formal relationship with the Nazi government, but conceded that the advice he offered his client was ultimately intended to guide the German government in its public relations in the United States. Among other things, he made suggestions for German statements on disarmament and also proposed that

Joachim von Rippentrop, the special commissioner for disarmament, should visit the U.S. to explain Germany's position to President Roosevelt and also to enlighten the Foreign Policy Association and the Council on Foreign Relations on the subject.

Lee testified that he disseminated no German propaganda here, that he only acted as an adviser, and that his advice included the repeated suggestion that "they could never in the world get the American people reconciled to their treatment of the Jews" and that Nazi propaganda in the U.S. was a mistake. But he never succeeded in establishing the ethics of taking money to advise a fascist government.

By the time we entered World War I, public relations had won a measure of acceptance from American corporations. Ivy Lee's success had also encouraged a number of competitors, among them his friend Pendleton Dudley, who opened his office in 1909. Now in his eighties, Dudley still presides over the affairs of Dudley-Anderson-Yutzy, one of the largest outfits in the business. Ivy Lee's office—known since 1933 as Ivy Lee and T. J. Ross—is still going strong, though Lee died in 1934.

During the first war, George Creel's Committee on Public Information was a training ground in the arts of propaganda for two energetic young men, Edward L. Bernays and Carl Byoir. Byoir, after an interval in trade, went on to become one of the most spectacular PR men of the modern era; Bernays became the ideologue of public relations and one of its shrewdest practitioners.

Public relations won more converts during the twenties. With the depression, the businessman suffered such a blow to his public esteem that the services of the new "profession" were in even greater demand. The business community desperately

needed a face lifting, an infusion of self-confidence, a new eloquence to move a heedless public.

The Carl Byoir office was established in 1930. In 1933, John
Hill came to New York to undertake an elaborate public relations program for the American Iron and Steel Institute. Today
the Byoir office and Hill and Knowlton are the largest firms in
PR. Earl Newsom opened his shop in 1935. Ben Sonnenberg,
who began as a press agent in the twenties, made the transition
into corporate public relations. Anna Rosenberg, fresh from her
first triumphs in government service, entered the field, as did
James Selvage, after several years beating the drums for Free
Private Enterprise under the auspices of the National Association
of Manufacturers. A flock of other hopefuls moved in.

At the same time, many large corporations started to set
up their own public relations departments. Bethlehem Steel
launched its operation in 1930, General Motors in 1931, U. S.
Steel in 1936, International Harvester in 1937, the Pittsburgh
Plate Glass Company and the New York Central Railroad in
1939.

In their politics, most of the recruits to PR were conservative,
a few liberal, some neutral with only a technician's passion for
the client's well-being. Their talent as image makers was well
rewarded. By the mid-1940's, three thousand dollars a month
was not an unusual sum for an outside consulting firm. Science
or art, engineering of consent paid better than either.

Luther Conant recalls the occasion, while he was working in
Edward Bernays' shop, when a staff member left to found his
own PR firm. "I wonder how he will make out," Conant said,
"he's so terribly shy."

"No reason why he cannot succeed," Bernays replied. "He'll

get the shy clients. Someone who is gregarious will attract the gregarious clients."

The observation was well taken. So varied are the personalities as well as the scope of independent PR firms that there can hardly be any quirks of executive character or special corporate requirements which cannot be accommodated. Large, substantial firms, heavy with dignity, are naturally attracted by the solid demeanor of Hill and Knowlton, Inc. A company in the market for a no-holds-barred publicity assault might well gravitate to Carl Byoir & Associates. A client who prizes sumptuous entertainment and engaging flattery is likely to find Ben Sonnenberg irresistible. Bernays will appeal to businessmen who enjoy sociological jargon.

The many hundreds of PR firms provide all sorts of services. There are general firms which try to cater to every corporate need. Others specialize—in financial PR, fashion publicity, entertainment press agentry, even so narrow a field as product publicity for pharmaceutical companies. Fund-raising is another specialized area. A few small operators support themselves doing public relations, and in some instances advertising as well, for trade unions. In California, Whitaker & Baxter and their competitors devote themselves to "professional" campaign management. This does not exhaust the categories.

Public relations companies differ greatly in size. They range from one-man shops to PR factories employing scores of people in offices around the country. Fees are equally variable—ranging from a subsistence wage for struggling newcomers to the fifty-thousand-dollars-a-year "entrance fee" which Byoir & Associates requires. A self-respecting firm, handling business accounts, will seldom admit that it charges less than a thousand dollars a month; but many small firms do. For a firm of any substance, two thousand dollars a month and up is quite common.

Fee systems follow no standard pattern. Some firms charge a flat fee, inclusive of expenses. Others charge a fee and bill a client separately for expenses. Still another system involves a retainer, a separate sum to cover the prorated salaries of employees on the account, and finally out-of-pocket expenses. Large and affluent firms follow this practice. A variant is to add an additional sum for overhead. Some firms also charge the client a commission—generally 15 per cent or 17½ per cent—on outside expenditures undertaken on his behalf. And the most fortunate PR men, in a period of rising equity values, are those relatively few individuals who have been able to receive part of their compensation in stock options.

The substantial firms will generally give a reporter accurate figures on fees and an accurate approximation of their volume of business. (A few will furnish no financial data whatsoever.) With smaller firms one can only speculate whether one is dealing with fact or wish fulfillment. And whether the firm is large or small, there is no independent source of verification for the figures. As for profits, the margins vary greatly and are not the sort of thing most gentlemen talk about. Profit figures would mean little anyway, for executive salaries and bonuses can fluctuate greatly from year to year.

The public relations field, in all its variety, inventiveness, flamboyance and solemn pretentiousness, can perhaps best be approached, at the outset, by an examination of a representative sampling of its hardiest practitioners—the independent consultants. First—Ben Sonnenberg.

2

Ben Sonnenberg:

the Art of

Dazzling

Clients

A visitor once asked Benjamin Sonnenberg exactly what he did for the clients of his public relations firm.

"That's easy," said Sonnenberg, meditatively stroking the ends of his walrus mustache. "Let's say there's a guy in New York who's the vice-president of a bank. He comes from a fine family. The family escutcheon was once a wondrous shining object, but now it has become slightly tarnished. Our client has gotten divorced a couple of times, he runs around with a fast crowd, his name appears in the tabloids. What I do for him is simple: I breathe on the family escutcheon—and he polishes while I breathe."

The discreet breath of Ben Sonnenberg is one of the more expensive vapors in Manhattan: "I would say that no one should think of me if he can't afford $5,000 a month" (a remark, like all of Sonnenberg's remarks, which is of course subject to revision for hyperbole). Other sources, even more reliable, indicate that his range of fees is between $36,000 and $50,000 a year plus expenses—for which a client gets Ben's advice and the workaday services of an account executive. Sonnenberg is expensive ("I'm like vintage wine") but by no means the most expensive PR man in New York.

Not all his clients, of course, require reburnished escutcheons. In his long career Sonnenberg has provided a variety of services for Charles Luckman, Juan Trippe, Prince Matchabelli, Grand Duchess Marie of Russia and Samuel Slotkin of Hygrade Food Products. As with most practitioners in the higher echelons of public relations, a Sonnenberg client is normally a corporation, but he naturally devotes much of his talents to its chief executive. Among his current clients are Philip Morris, Greyhound Bus, Stouffer's, U. S. Industries, Automatic Canteen Company of America, T. J. Lipton and Associated Dry Goods.

Sonnenberg has also become one of his own best clients. He insists that he does not seek personal publicity, though he has devoted much of his career to fabricating a personality which inevitably elicits attention. His motives have been understandable: to attract potential clients, to impress present clients and to revel in his own legend.

In the literal sense of the word, he is a self-made man: there was nothing quite like Ben Sonnenberg, in the gaudy world of publicity, until he began to live his fantasies. He is worth more than a passing glance, however, for his flamboyance is atypical only in that it is inflated to heroic dimensions. In modest scale, the Sonnenberg method can be seen as a significant strand in many PR operations.

Shorn of adornments (which only occurs in the privacy of his closet: he is dressed even on the beach), Sonnenberg is short, bald-headed, rotund. Clothed for action, he is an impressive sight—with his luxuriant mustache, four-buttoned jacket, colored bib-front shirt, solid knitted tie and cuff links made of huge coins. In winter he wears a derby or Homburg, in summer a boater, in all seasons he is a picture of Edwardian splendor.

He lives in a style befitting his haberdashery—in a huge elegant house in New York's Gramercy Park, which used to be owned by Mrs. Stuyvesant Fish. It is typical of Sonnenberg that one large, five-story house was too modest for his needs; he actually occupies two adjoining buildings, which he combined into one some years ago.

The Sonnenberg establishment, staffed by six servants, is a turn-of-the-century extravaganza crammed with gleaming brass, huge chandeliers, miles of wall paneling, oils, displays of expensive chinaware, endless rows of books, a bust of Disraeli, and a kitchen that could service a small hotel. Ben's particular pride is a private movie theater on the top floor.

"Not bad, eh, for a boy from Grand Street?" he is likely to observe, nestling his slippered feet into the damask cushion and rolling his brandy in a huge snifter.

His conversational style has the same relaxed ostentation— long circuitous rambles, slightly patronizing, with sudden disarming eruptions of self-mockery. "If you want to know the secret of my career," says Sonnenberg, "it is simply this: I have a quality many publicity men don't have—I have warmth. The thing is to approach life with warmth, to approach it affirmatively. I have enthusiasm, I can communicate enthusiasm. I can make you read a book or see a play. I run the best salon in New York, I know the alchemy of people.

"If I had Guy de Rothschild to dinner, I wouldn't try to find richer men for guests. I'd ask people richer than him in public displacement, in by-line value. My idea of who to put against

Guy de Rothschild would be Gunther, Murrow. If I want to
send you a present—and you're a great big lug—I'll send you a
leather-bound edition of Cellini. I don't trade down, I trade up.
You hire me if you're looking for a measure of social responsibility, for a higher batting average, and because you want a brain
truster who knows the climate of the hour."

An example of his work? That is difficult; he hates to be
specific about the daily grind. "I'd be glad to recite a hundred
failures to you. Not every girl whom I've propositioned has succumbed. I have been rebuffed, fired, negated, jettisoned. But I
have that capacity for rationalization that only a man five feet
seven possesses—I know that the girls who rejected me didn't
have good taste, that the clients who refused me couldn't hear
my Wagnerian trumpets."

How did he get where he is today? "This is the way I'd like
it to read—I was born the illegitimate son of Franz Joseph. My
mother was the great prima donna." But, sadly, he confesses that
his father did indeed run a clothing store on Grand Street, on
New York's impoverished lower East Side. Ben was born in
Brest-Litovsk, Poland, on July 12, 1901, came to this country as a
child. In his teens, he was one of the prize exhibits of the Henry
Street Settlement, where he met his future wife, Hilda Caplan,
and so impressed Lillian Wald that she helped him get a scholarship to Columbia. He studied journalism for a bit, then threw
up college to go to work. "I was a restless kid," he says.

He sold portraits in the Midwest, worked a few months on the
Flint, Michigan, *Journal*, returned to New York to write press
releases for the Joint Distribution Committee. Then came an
opportunity to work for Hoover's American Relief Administration, distributing food in the Ukraine. (Lillian Wald recommended him to Lewis Strauss, who gave him the job.) He spent

six months in the Ukraine, lived well in a villa near Odessa. With his dollar savings, he took a swing around Europe, finding the high life dirt cheap. As he later told *The New Yorker's* Geoffrey Hellman:

"The significance of having a man draw your bath and lay out your clothes burst upon me like a revelation. I realized for the first time what it was to be rich. I took a tintype in my mind of the way I wanted to be—a bon vivant, a patron of the arts, a man who could mix Picasso with Dun and Bradstreet."

In pursuit of this ambition he came home and in 1924 became a press agent, starting on Broadway, moving on to hotel accounts, fashion, and finally, in the 1930's, making the decisive leap to corporate clients.

The Sonnenberg operation cannot be understood without reference to his props—clothes, house, elegant lunches at such establishments as "21," Le Pavillon and the Colony. For there is a seamless quality to Sonnenberg's life—absolutely no separation between work and play. His shop (he has around twenty-five employees, two or three of whom earn thirty thousand a year or more) turns out a competent publicity product, but what distinguishes his endeavor is the personal flourish.

He is very adept at handling the press. His stock in trade is exuberant flattery, delivered with an engaging air of roguish humor. A reporter will phone him with a query, and Sonnenberg will explode boisterously, "Goddam it! I thought you were calling to say you had resigned so that I could hire you at triple your salary." Let the reporter run into Sonnenberg in a restaurant, and he finds himself introduced to the assembled throng as a young man on whom the mantle of Pulitzer or Luce is likely to fall.

The seductive Sonnenberg seldom ends an amiable interview

with a reporter without the good-humored suggestion that the next meeting, perhaps, should be in Paris or the Bahamas. One can almost see the plane ticket poking out of Ben's inside pocket; according to rumor in the trade, more than one reporter has succumbed.

With more modest gifts there is no subterfuge. "You ought to interveiw my tailor," says Sonnenberg, "and while you're there—say!—I'll have him make you a handsome Norfolk jacket." When the offer is declined, Sonnenberg's guard goes up.

Though some reporters regard him with suspicion, there is no evidence that the interests of Sonnenberg's clients have suffered. Indeed, at times he has perhaps been too successful in publicizing his charges. The classic instance involved wonder boy Charles Luckman, into whose life Sonnenberg came when he got the Pepsodent account in 1939. Pepsodent was later bought out by Lever Bros., and in 1946 Luckman became head of the parent firm. Sonnenberg was at his elbow throughout, directing one of the fabulous press build-ups of the postwar era.

Luckman had been a Republican; Sonnenberg helped transform him into a liberal with evident Fair Deal sympathies. The "liberal businessman" is sufficiently novel to provide a useful switch; it may involve corporate complications, but it usually gets a good press. Before long Luckman appeared on the cover of *Time;* signed pieces by him were published in *Collier's, Harper's* and other magazines; he went up and down the land orating to rapturous audiences. He criticized businessmen for their hostility to social reforms, criticized labor unions for poor working conditions in their own shops—headline-catching copy in each case.

In 1947, President Truman drafted Luckman—by this time probably the best-known salesman in the land—to head up a voluntary food drive, designed to get Americans to eat less so that we could export more to Europe. Luckman also served on Truman's Committee on Civil Rights, helped boom the Freedom Train.

His public relations could hardly have been better, but things were not going well back at the Lever shop. Luckman had made some unfortunate business decisions, had a few bad breaks as well, and early in 1950 suddenly lost his job. Ben, however, had done his own job very well.

Sonnenberg provides more than ingenious press agentry; some clients highly prize his counsel. The counseling function is closeted in Sonnenberg's ornate, dark-wooded office far down the corridor from his publicity factory, where the appointments are crisp and functional. In back of a massive desk sits Sonnenberg, bubbling away genially. To his right, sitting inconspicuously next to the wall, is his long-time colleague, George Schreiber, a voluble, mildly agitated man who dresses in rumpled clothes and has spent many years blinking in the glare surrounding Sonnenberg. Schreiber is a nonpracticing lawyer ("a Harvard Law School graduate," Ben tells visitors, with proprietary pride) and his function, among other things, is to restrain Sonnenberg's impetuosity.

They are an effective team. One admirer is George Weissman, an alumnus of Sonnenberg's shop who is now—as director of marketing for Philip Morris—a Very Important Client. "Ben and George paint a broader picture with a broader brush than most of the old-line practitioners," says Weissman. "With them, the discussion is not only the usual PR stuff about 'the various publics,' but it covers your sales problems, your over-all corporate policies, national politics, world trends."

Sonnenberg has had the Philip Morris account since the thirties, and Weissman credits him with developing, early in the game, the image of "a forward-looking, aggressive management" doing battle against the giant tobacco companies. In an industry where the product is pretty much the same, the over-all corporate reputation can have an eventual impact on sales, Weissman contends.

"Ben worked out the Philip Morris concept with Al Lyon, chairman of the board, and others. Basically, it was the concept of substituting good will for dollars, which we did not have. What was done concretely? Well, throughout the thirties, Philip Morris wouldn't cut retail prices, unlike our competitors. We had no two packs for twenty-five cents. As a result, we had the whole trade pushing us. This was no decision of Ben's, but part of the concept. The company recognized the importance of opinion leaders; we were the first to hire college students to give out small packs of samples. The company has always had the best labor relations in the industry—which was probably due to Ben's influence."

And of course, with Sonnenberg's diligent assistance, the corporation had no end of agreeable publicity. Weissman rattles off *Forbes, Business Week, Newsweek,* the *Wall Street Journal,* the New York *Times* and *Fortune* as publications which have celebrated the exploits of his company. "We've had two pieces in *Fortune,*" he boasts. This sort of thing helps the sale of stock. In recent years, when Philip Morris launched an advertising campaign in behalf of the "Marlboro man" and the flip-top box, Sonnenberg went to imaginative lengths to publicize this newest thrust of the forward-looking, aggressive management.

"We got tremendous amounts of publicity—in columns, in magazines, in the trade press, in Broadway shows," Weissman reports. "In fact, one of Ben's operators even got Zsa Zsa Gabor to say to an interviewer that her ambition was to be the Marlboro woman!"

Triumph indeed, and yet another example of how many-sided are the talents required of even the PR man who operates on the highest corporate levels. His detractors, of course, suggest that Sonnenberg is nothing more than a press agent. Sonnenberg does not disdain the term. Instead he has a genial contempt for the solemnity of the "professional" PR types and will not join their organizations.

To a great extent his success comes from his ability to persuade his clients that with Sonnenberg they get press agentry flavored with the elegance of a world they never knew. Many clients look down on their press agents; Sonnenberg makes them look up. His operation is interesting as a study in the techniques of dazzling clients quite as much as in the techniques of public relations.

In much of public relations, after all, there is a certain intangible quality: is it worth many thousands a year, for example, to win the immortality of a cover on *Time*, a "Talk" piece in *The New Yorker* and several encomiums in the trade press?

Whether it is or not, Sonnenberg, at least, has an uncanny ability to persuade his admirers that he is worth his fee just to be available at the other end of the phone. He has few equals, in New York, as a telephone performer.

"How do I get clients?" says Sonnenberg. "By traversing the lanes of traffic." To his intimates he has sometimes been franker. "Before I met Albert Lasker," he once remarked, "I was always seen with beautiful blondes. After I met Albert Lasker, I was always seen with Albert Lasker."

A bit of exaggeration, perhaps, but the reflected glory of Lasker, who made a great fortune in advertising, certainly enhanced Sonnenberg's luster in the eyes of prospective clients.

From his earliest years Sonnenberg understood the value of a good front. When he first moved into the Gramercy Park house he could only afford to occupy the first two floors. "But you had no periscope to see that I didn't have the rest of the house," Sonnenberg points out. Since then the house has infinitely aided his "public relations posture." With one visit to his establishment, says Sonnenberg, "the prospect sees that I'm no fly-by-night. I may have more money than he has, and I may well have been operating at this stand longer than he has been president of his company."

He is frank to confess that he has other assets, as well. "I know the difference between Isaiah Berlin and Irving Berlin and I know them both. I lunch in the bar of the Pavillon, I prefer that. You'll find me at '21' and the Racquet Club. Bob Dowling sends me four tickets to the opening of the Lunt play—row B—and I don't have to pay for them. You see, one maintains a certain posture."

And one attracts and keeps clients by doing them a multitude of favors—theater tickets, hotel rooms during the World Series, reservations at chi-chi restaurants. (To his clients, he prefers to give the impression that he never pays for theater tickets.)

For the Midwest businessman eager to meet the elite of New York, Sonnenberg will throw an *intime* dinner for twenty, with a guest list containing three or four authors, a celebrated painter, a pair of movie actresses, prominent lawyers, government officials and investment bankers. At nine-thirty another sixty citizens troop in for drinks, a movie and a midnight snack. Almost everybody is some sort of "name." How many press agents can do that?

The client, of course, has no way of knowing how many other

New Yorkers did not accept Sonnenberg's invitations—out of an understandable reluctance to dress up a salon for commercial purposes. But enough do come so that in season Ben's home is often as well populated as the lobby of the Plaza.

Once a client retains him, Sonnenberg often plays a remarkable role—confidant, father surrogate, adviser on all manner of problems, personal as well as corporate. Jay Scott, who worked for Sonnenberg for years, recalls the time when a *nouveau riche* Midwest client showed up in Sonnenberg's office. "The guy was a big success. He had parlayed a few hundred thousand to nineteen million dollars, and Sonnenberg had a date all set up for him with a *Time* editor. And this character comes walking into Ben's office wearing a pair of black and white shoes."

Sonnenberg couldn't conceal his dismay. "Here I've been telling people what a sophisticated guy you are," he exclaimed, "and you don't know what kind of shoes to wear! Go out and buy yourself a pair of black shoes."

The client left immediately and returned shod in black.

On another occasion a client called to ask what Sonnenberg thought of his buying a seventy-five-hundred-dollar mink coat for a girl friend, a young lady then starring in a musical.

Snapped Ben: "I've been married twenty-five years and I've never bought my wife a seventy-five-hundred-dollar mink coat. You're silly!" And hung up.

The next day the client called back, apologetically, and said that of course Ben was right.

Sonnenberg's irreverence and his rigidities, because they are so in character, seldom offend. Unlike many of his competitors, he refuses to make "presentations"—elaborate programming of future PR campaigns—to prospective clients. "I'm an artist, not an accountant," he says stiffly. He prefers to meet in quiet séance with the top boss of the client firm, hates the committee system. He once sat through a luncheon with several high executives of the American Export Line, an important client, then walked out long before the session was over. He couldn't abide the boredom.

He can also afford to be selective about his clients. He turned down an account offered by Howard Hughes—because he did not relish having his sleep interrupted by long-distance calls from the eccentric millionaire, who is famous for never finishing the day before dawn.

"With Ben, you have to stimulate him and cajole him and enchant him," George Weissman points out. "This is a very temperamental artist at times—and he responds to all the techniques he uses on his clients. Two days ago, I had lunch with Ben and had to give him hell for the things his staff hadn't followed through on. Today there was a phone call from him and he ticked off everything that had been done."

Sonnenberg hardly regards client relations as a simple matter. "There is a touch of chemistry to it—it's like a marriage—you get acquainted, you get grafted on to one another, there are calms and crises."

But he has a deft touch in a crisis. He received word one day that an aggrieved client was on his way to see him. Sonnenberg swept open the door for his visitor, sat him down and fixed him with a doleful eye. "I know, I know," he said mournfully. "I took your money. I didn't deliver. I was no good. I cheated you."

"Ben, hold on!" the client exclaimed. "You're not that bad! I just had a few suggestions to make." Ben was inconsolable—until the full dramatic impact was scored—then they quickly came to a meeting of minds.

He is fond of saying, "Other men collect antiques; I collect rich men." He collects both, of course—as well as numbers of individuals with relatively little money but the sort of "public displacement" which may one day be valuable to him. Typical was his pursuit of David Schoenbrun, the well-known CBS chief correspondent in Paris. Sonnenberg was introduced to Schoenbrun a few years ago in Paris and ever since has been soliciting his good favor. "I flew into New York from Paris," says Schoenbrun, "and there was immediately a call at the hotel from Sonnenberg. 'What do you like—a blonde, a brunette or a redhead?' he asked in his kidding way. I told him that I was in love with my wife. The next trip to New York, when my wife was with me, Ben's secretary called to say that unfortunately Mr. Sonnenberg was out of town, but he wanted to send us two theater tickets each night of my stay. What shows did I want to see? I explained that I wasn't interested in going to the theater, whereupon she said that she would select the shows. And every day two tickets arrived."

Never once did Sonnenberg ask a plug for a client. Indeed, the only time he requested a favor was one day in Paris when he took Schoenbrun to lunch. "All through lunch I was curious about this tall parcel that Ben had beside his chair," Schoenbrun recalls, "but he made no reference to it. At the end of the meal, he undid the wrapping and unveiled a four-foot pile of my book, *As France Goes*. He thought so highly of it that he was sending copies to all his friends. How could I help but be flattered? All he wanted—clever fellow—was that I autograph the copies with greetings to each recipient. I told him I'd sign my own name, but no more. *He'd* have to write in his friends' names himself." Despite the rebuff, Sonnenberg remained as cordial as ever.

But Sonnenberg is unwilling to waste his efforts on unpromising material. An acquaintance of both men remembers the occasion, years ago, when Sonnenberg had lunch at "21" with Robert Ruark, who was then an obscure newspaperman.

"Tell me, Bob," said Sonnenberg, "are you going to be successful in this town?"

"I hope so," said Ruark.

"If you're not, I'm not going to cultivate you," Sonnenberg warned.

Of such is the stuff of the Sonnenberg legend. Sonnenberg's practice of public relations, as a British admirer, Lord Kinross, noted not long ago, is very much a matter of private relations. Kinross, who arrived in New York with an introduction from a London friend, was given the "A" treatment by Sonnenberg—tea with the master, party invitations, tickets, newspaper clippings which might interest him, letters of introduction—topped off by attendance at the twenty-fifth dinner of the Lucullus Circle at the Waldorf Astoria (gold plate to eat off, "priceless tapestries" on the wall, more than a dozen different types of wine). When he returned home, Lord Kinross wrote a newspaper tribute to "this expansive Benjamin from somewhere in Central Europe" who had invented public relations.

A little poetic exaggeration, worthy of expansive Benjamin himself, who promptly photostated the article and shipped it around to his admirers.

3

Bernays:

Ideologue

Engineering

Consent

To Edward L. Bernays goes the distinction of being the first and doubtless the leading ideologue of public relations. He codified the concepts which have since become the clichés. If Ben Sonnenberg exemplifies the more flamboyant aspects of PR, Bernays epitomizes its wistful yearnings for scholarly distinction. He is also one of the few early missionaries still doing business under the old tent. And he has made a fortune.

"The secret of Eddie Bernays' success," one of his clients once observed, "is simply talk. The man just swamps you in a morass of rhetoric. I hired him to convince my board of directors of the value of public relations. When I finally mastered the patter myself, I had no further need of him."

Bernays, now in his late sixties, is a short, plumpish man with a grizzled mustache and an air of benign assurance. Addressing a client or a reporter, he displays the tolerant, unruffled manner of the psychoanalyst—an appropriate resemblance, for Bernays' proudest family connection was the late Sigmund Freud, his uncle, and Bernays himself, according to friends, likes to think of himself as a kind of psychoanalyst to troubled corporations.

He talks, of course, far more than a psychoanalyst. As he meditatively pats his paunch, his most characteristic gesture, the words tumble forth in an endless cascade, the polysyllables lulling the auditor's critical faculties, the clods of jargon dropping like huge pillows which cushion the mind against anxiety. At times one has only a dim view of what Bernays is saying, but it sounds great. "I got so I could write the stuff myself," says Morris M. Lee, Jr., a former staff member, "but I could never understand it."

In print, Bernays' conversational style is less impressive, but an example or two may suggest its quality.

"The counsel on public relations," Bernays once remarked to this reporter, "is what sociologists call a societal technician who is fitted by training and experience to evaluate the maladjustments and adjustments between his client and the publics upon whom the client is dependent for his socially sound activity." (Who does the client turn to, one wonders, for his socially unsound activity?)

Explaining, on another occasion, why he has rejected certain clients (like the purveyors of patent medicines), Bernays said, "I wouldn't want it on my superego that I did for money what I wouldn't do without money." The rule, apparently, is that one never uses a prosaic word like "conscience" when a Freudian neologism will do instead.

Bernays, without question, is one of the greatest salesmen public relations has ever seen. "If you listen to him long enough," says an old associate, "he'll eventually mesmerize you into doing anything he wants." Over the years, he has mesmerized the managements of such diverse groups as the United Fruit Company, Procter & Gamble, Beech-Nut, Mack Truck, Philco, American Tobacco, *McCall's* magazine, GM, GE and the American Nurses Association.

The hypnotic relationship, one gathers, was of great psychic pleasure to the clients and of considerable benefit, financial and spiritual, to Bernays. He is surprisingly reticent about his fees, but he is willing to concede that he once received as much as $100,000 for two months' work and $1,000 for a mere hour's advice. Former employees, who worked for Bernays at the height of his activity (his shop is much quieter now), say that his standard fee was $50,000 a year, plus a pro rata charge for staff salaries, though he sometimes took less. In any event, he has made more than enough money to be able to afford, on occasion, a free proffering of his counsel to do-good groups.

In the trade he is regarded as the man who has probably done more than anyone else to "professionalize" public relations. He claims to have been the first to use the term "counsel on public relations," in 1921. Two years later, Bernays published the first book on the subject, *Crystallizing Public Opinion,* taught the first university course—at New York University.

Crystallizing Public Opinion, among other things, provided an elevated definition of the public relations counsel "as one who directs and supervises the activities of his clients wherever they impinge upon the daily life of the public. He interprets the client to the public, which he is enabled to do in part because he interprets the public to the client. His advice is given on all occasions on which his client appears before the public . . ."

The implication, so congenial to a new and insecure calling, was that the PR counsel's advice was also likely to be taken on all occasions. This deference was deserved, for the PR counsel, in Bernays' view, had to meet an exacting set of qualifications: he is "first of all a student. His field of study is the public mind. His text books for this study are the facts of life; the articles printed in newspapers and magazines . . . the speeches that are delivered in legislative chambers, the sermons issuing from pulpits, anecdotes related in smoking rooms, the gossip of Wall Street, the patter of the theater and the conversation of other men who, like him, are interpreters and must listen for the clear or obscure enunciations of the public." One is left with the image of Bernays scurrying from Wall Street to theater to smoking room, so busy soaking up public enunciations that he has barely time to phone advice to his clients.

Several threads can be followed through the ponderous corpus of Bernays' theoretical work. He has long argued eloquently that public relations was far more than mere press agentry. Publicity was only the final outcome of a complex canvassing of the client's problems, surveying of his public image, restructuring of his thinking and reshaping of his corporate façade.

In considerable detail, he elaborated the thought offered by Ivy Lee that good publicity must involve deeds as well as words on the client's part. Bernays spent much time analyzing the constituents of the public which he was trying to influence, concluding that crowd psychology was far different from individual psychology and that "the public" was made up of a web of disparate publics, to each of which one often had to appeal. He devoted much thought to "group leaders," their effect on the unthinking herd and the methods by which they could be reached. The irrational element in man, and how it could be appealed to for the client's benefit, was a central preoccupation. From the outset, Bernays also stressed the value of "creating events"—

an award, a well-publicized "scientific" survey, a symposium, a banquet, indeed anything that would endow a client with some news value.

Crystallizing Public Opinion was at least an innocuous title. On occasion the tag was more candid; in 1928 Bernays published an essay called "Manipulating Public Opinion." On the other hand, he often stressed the ethical restraints incumbent on the practitioner. To give his all for a client, the PR counsel was not obliged to believe in his client's case; at the same time, he was constrained not to do anything inimical to society.

The ethical practitioner, in his emphatic view, was more than a neutral figure. He provided a distinct public service, for an interesting reason. All the techniques of public relations, Bernays argued, were available to minority as well as majority groups in the community. Hence the PR man could be very helpful in breaking up conformist patterns of thought and winning acceptance for new ideas. Indeed, in one of his more euphoric moments, Bernays suggested that it was the ultimate job of the PR counsel to create a "public conscience."

Like many of his followers, Bernays came to public relations through entertainment press agentry. A 1912 product of the Cornell Agricultural College, he first broke into print in the *Dietetic and Hygiene Gazette* and the *Medical Review of Reviews*. He was a competent medical journalist, but found his true metier when he started writing press puffs for such celebrated clients as Caruso, Henry Miller, Otis Skinner and the Diaghileff Russian Ballet. There followed a period of service, during World War I, with George Creel's Committee on Public Information, a valuable training ground in the arts of propaganda.

In 1918, Bernays had an encounter with history because of a

conversation with Thomas Masaryk, the founder of the new Czechoslovak Republic, at Delmonico's restaurant in New York. Masaryk told Bernays that the announcement of the independence of his country was to be made on a Sunday in October. Bernays demurred: the event was likely to be buried in the Sunday papers, where there was so much competing news. Better hold off the announcement for Monday morning, when news was usually light. Masaryk was dismayed at so opportunist a maneuver, but he was won over. And thus to the young press agent fell the surprising honor of naming Czechoslovakia's independence day.

In 1919, Bernays set up his own shop. Three years later he married his assistant, Doris E. Fleischman, and she has been his partner ever since. The venture in matrimony also launched the partners in a well-publicized crusade to establish Miss Fleischman's right to her maiden name. Bernays had helped found the Lucy Stoner League and he was all for his wife's effort to register with him at a hotel as "Doris E. Fleischman, wife." A great *brouhaha* was caused by their successful efforts to get New York's Health Department to concede that a child could be legitimate even though the mother's maiden name appeared on the birth certificate.

Despite these hijinks, clients regarded Bernays as a very sound fellow. He was effective in client relations in large part because his prescription, stripped of his rococo verbalisms, was a reasonably simple, and indeed sensible, one. A former employee, who lacks the master's stylistic grace, has put it succinctly:

"First, find out what the public thinks of you (a survey is the standard prescription); second, examine what you really are; third, bridge the gap in one of two ways—either change what you are or change the conception." To be most effective, of course, the changes should be subtle and oblique. The Bernays approach, which is now standard PR practice in many types of campaigns, is to woo the public in ways which it can hardly detect.

Some years ago, for example, Procter & Gamble was troubled by a boycott of Negro customers. Their grievance was well known—a radio soap commercial spoken, in offensive Mammy dialect, by a Negro washerwoman. Alarmed at this breach in its public relations, P & G eagerly sought Bernays' counsel.

He suggested, quite sensibly, that they change the commercial but also do a good deal more—hire Negroes in other than menial jobs in their Cincinnati plant, print the pictures of Negro employees in their house organ, invite Negroes to "open house" days at the plant. Word of such enlightenment, which Bernays did not propose to publicize in any overt way, would gradually seep through the Negro community and affect the attitude of soap purchasers. P & G bought the prescription, but objected to eliminating the commercial; it drew well with the white trade. In the end, however, the commercial was toned down. The boycott eventually evaporated; and once again, in his celebrated phrase, Bernays had "engineered the consent" of a fractious public.

In another instance related by an old Bernays hand (Bernays himself will only attach names to ancient case histories), the Columbian Rope Company sought his help, some years ago, to fight an obstreperous union. The Columbian people had seen one of the full-page institutional ads which Bernays used to publish in the New York *Times*—this one dealing with the creation of sound labor relations—but they somehow had failed to get the message.

Bernays would have none of union-busting (he is a liberal, after all, in his own societal impulses). "But I'll help you live with the union," he offered brightly—and proceeded to the lecture. In the end, he persuaded the rope people.

Thereafter, his first step was a survey, which showed that the company was regarded in its community with considerable hostility. Then came an elaborate program: a weekly radio show, with live entertainment and little chats by labor and management people; a new open-house policy, to show towns-folk the plant; sponsorship with the department of education of a vocational guidance conference for the entire county; and various other projects to prove that the company was a good citizen. It also, of course, bargained with its union.

The Bernays effort had its anticipated result: labor relations were improved, and the client's public image was transformed into a thing of glowing benignity. After a couple of years, however, the experiment was dropped, for the company head was troubled about the change in his private image. He complained that the boys in the club had taken to calling him "Sir Galahad." Before this obstacle, Bernays was helpless.

At times, his prescription seems surprisingly elementary; one wonders why the client did not think of it himself. A nationally known hat company complained that its product was not going over well with the Negro trade, though it advertised in the Negro press. Bernays pondered long and hard and finally diagnosed the problem: his client was showing white models in his ads. Negro models were thereafter employed. Sales increased.

Burnishing the personal exterior of an otherwise uncelebrated client is another Bernays specialty. One of his client corporations was being threatened by a raid by a fast-rising financier. The assault centered in large part on a disparagement of the talents of the company's chief executive. Bernays did not waste time on defending a fixed position, but moved to the offensive. He persuaded a professional engineering group of the outstanding achievements of his client, won him an award. The honor was duly celebrated in the press and insistently drawn to the attention of the stockholders. The raid was fended off.

Much of Bernays' "engineering of consent" has been undertaken with the simple goal of moving merchandise. For Venida hair nets, early in his career, he promoted the notion in all media that loose hair was a health and safety hazard; as a result of his efforts, several states passed laws requiring waitresses and female factory workers to wear hair nets—thereby selling more nets and adding to the "public visibility" of the client's product.

For Procter & Gamble, he got a plethora of free publicity (and sold a lot of soap) by starting a nationwide soap modeling contest in the schools.

For the Beech-Nut Packing Company, he promoted the sale of bacon not by booming his client's name but by mounting a propaganda drive in behalf of the hearty breakfast. Here, unquestionably, we have the coincidence of the public and private interest of which PR men like to speak, for how can nutrition not be in the public interest?

For the Golden Jubilee of the electric light, back in 1929, Bernays carried off one of the great publicity coups of the era, with Edison re-enacting his discovery under Henry Ford's sponsorship in Dearborn, an event attended by President Hoover and commemorated by a special stamp issued by the post office department. To a press agent, it was a highly successful stunt; to Bernays it was an "overt act."

Many years ago, as Bernays relates in his book *Public Relations,* he brought the "overt act technique" right into the White

House. In 1924 Bernays was involved with the Non-Partisan Committee for the re-election of Calvin Coolidge. The problem was to persuade the country that "silent Cal" was a warm, likable human being and not the cold fish his detractors portrayed. Searching for a "dramatic way" to transform Coolidge's image, his backers decided that he should entertain a group of movie and stage stars at a White House breakfast. Al Jolson, Charlotte Greenwood, the Dolly Sisters and several others were recruited for the homey griddle-cake session, and the event was prominently chronicled on front pages across the land. It set a precedent, Bernays reports proudly, for never before had a U.S. President invited actors to breakfast.

Over the years Bernays has also devoted a good deal of time to the public relations of Edward L. Bernays. This has largely taken the form of an enormous outpouring of speeches, articles, books and advertisements on the history and methodology of public relations, with candid attention to the contributions thereto of E.L.B. Certainly no man has propagandized more ardently in behalf of the new discipline, a fact which has not gone unrecorded by the nation's press. Ex-staff-members report that each batch of clippings, heralding another of his speeches or articles, would suffuse him with a warm glow of contentment. One former associate recalls a standard ritual: first thing in the morning, Bernays would call him in, toss a flattering clipping across the desk, and exclaim happily, as he patted his midriff, "Sets up the ego for the day!"

Major sustenance for the ego was provided, some years ago, by an elaborate printed bibliography of his career which Bernays distributed widely. The book, entitled *Public Relations, Edward L. Bernays and the American Scene,* is a work of eighty-six closely printed, two-column pages which describes every public utterance by Bernays and every fleeting reference to his activities in the works of others.

In the first category are such memorable items as his contribution to the *Wellesley College News* in 1946 ("Bernays Urges College Students to Help Create Peaceful World"), an appearance in the *New York State Pharmacist* in 1943, an article in the *Southern Lumberman* in 1946 ("ELB applies public relations principles to problems of lumber industry") as well as essays in weightier journals like the *Public Opinion Quarterly* and the *Yale Review*. On occasion, even editorial notes accompanying his articles are immortalized (e.g., from the *New Leader*, "Edward L. Bernays is one of America's leading public relations counsels").

The second category, "Writings About Edward L. Bernays," covers an even broader expanse. Books which merely listed works by Bernays in *their* bibliographies are reciprocally listed in *his*; an author who included Bernays in her acknowledgments in turn finds her own work acknowledged; a book which "indirectly" quoted Bernays is duly rescued from obscurity, as are novels in which Bernays is mentioned in passing. (Among them, *For Immediate Release* by Rion Bercovici, whose press-agent hero is quoted as asking: "What has Bernays got that I haven't got?")

In recent years, Bernays has been perpetrating fewer overt acts. He no longer employs a staff of writers, no longer even sends out press releases on behalf of clients (he sends them out frequently on behalf of his own "public service" projects, however). His professional work is devoted exclusively to advising clients. Fewer payroll costs that way, he explains, and you make as much if not more money. "Besides," he suggests, "after the first hundred thousand you only keep 9 per cent anyway."

To a reporter, oddly enough, he will not tell whom he advises or how many clients he has—a reticence, as Bernays might well advise a client, which can only lead to unflattering suspicions.

He maintains that his present setup has long been the one he wanted. From the outset of his career, he says, "I set out to create a doctor's office, not a Mayo clinic." It was only because of his clients' insistence on PR "operations" as well as counsel that he was forced to recruit a staff of writers. Ex-employees, however, cynically suggest that Bernays never wanted to build a large organization because he was not disposed to share the glory with colleagues, apart from his wife. When he did employ writers, the turnover was always high. One staff member, who remained for five years, kept a list of the people who worked for Bernays during that period. No more than 30 were employed at any one time, yet 270 individuals passed through the shop.

Life with Bernays was always more hazardous than in most PR offices. He enjoyed recruiting young men, to whom he would paint a bright picture of their future careers in public relations. Old employees agree that he was an excellent teacher. But one or two blunders—and, even worse, a disagreement with Bernays —brought instant dismissal. The actual firing was delegated to his office manager. On the other hand, Bernays took it as a personal affront when a staff member resigned. One writer, whose services were highly prized, announced one day that he was leaving in three weeks to set up his own firm. Bernays never spoke to him again.

The consequence of high turnover, of course, is that Bernays has probably trained more PR men than any other practitioner around. He has become a legend in his own time, though not perhaps in the way he intended. Meantime, he reigns serenely in his book-lined office in "Bernays House," a converted residence on Manhattan's East 64th Street, reading and advising clients the full day long. He does not eat lunch, has even been known to get his hair clipped in the office.

He welcomes an inquiring reporter, but his passion is to talk about the theory of public relations—not the mundane operations of his office and certainly not about money. "I never felt that money was the end of this activity," says Bernays. "I saw it as a socially useful function—and society has been very good to me."

4

Whitaker & Baxter: Political Pitchmen

In the weeks before the November 1958 election, a menacing-looking monkey wrench suddenly became a political weapon in California. The unlovely object was flung across billboards, newspaper ads, garish handbills—accompanied by the slogan, "Defeat the Monkey Wrench Tax Bill. Vote No on 17."

Proposition 17, in point of fact, was a complex measure which proposed to rejigger the state's tax system by reducing the sales tax, lowering income tax rates on modest incomes, raising them to 46 per cent on incomes over fifty thousand dollars. The measure was of doubtful wisdom, to put it mildly, but it was not precisely a monkey wrench either.

The monkey wrench motif, and the "fear campaign" which it dominated, bore the unmistakable touch of Whitaker & Baxter, the remarkable San Francisco husband-and-wife team who have long been the country's outstanding specialists in political public relations. They were the first in the field in the early thirties, have since run eighty major campaigns—winning all but six. In the last dozen years, they have paid personal income taxes on over a million dollars. The AMA alone paid them a fee of $350,000 for a strenuous crusade against compulsory medical insurance.

Their performance in the 1958 election measured up to the Whitaker & Baxter legend. Proposition 17 was defeated after a brilliantly executed campaign that threatened Californians with the wreckage of the state's entire financial structure and—what was perhaps even worse—the imposition of burdensome new taxes on food, real estate, gasoline if the Monkey Wrench was passed. While they conducted this crusade in northern California, Whitaker & Baxter also found time to handle a successful statewide campaign for Proposition 4—a sixty-million-dollar harbor bond issue—as well as to run Governor Knight for U.S. senator. They resigned the Knight campaign after the primary; he lost in the November general election.

By 1958, Clem Whitaker and Leone Baxter had been fixtures of California politics far longer than anyone in high state office. At the end of the year, however, they retired from active involvement in purely California campaigns to devote themselves to "counseling" national and foreign clients on how to run similar crusades. They sold their California firm, Campaigns, Inc., to their three junior partners—James Dorais, Clem Whitaker, Jr. and Newton Stearns, who continue at the old stand, with the old customers, using the well-tested techniques and still calling the operation Whitaker & Baxter. Meantime, Clem and Leone personally carry on as Whitaker and Baxter, International.

After years in the business, the couple have lost none of their energy. Clem Whitaker is a tall, spindly man with a deeply lined, craggy face who looks older than his sixty years. He is something of a nonstop talker in a low, well-modulated voice that is oddly reassuring. Wife Leone Baxter, who is in her early fifties but looks surprisingly youthful, is a pretty redhead with the well-scrubbed, glowing complexion of the ageless American girl. She, too, is never at a loss for words, though her tone is sprightlier and she often sounds on the edge of a breathless discovery.

For a pair of old pros, Whitaker & Baxter are full of surprises. They relish talking about their coups but betray little of the cynicism of the veteran politico. In their view, professional campaign management is an ennobling effort to raise the level of political awareness in a democracy. "We feel," Whitaker says solemnly, "that people in our state are better informed, more alive to the issues, are better citizens because of our type of activity."

They carry on these educational chores in close unison. At work, in the offices they occupied for years in the Flood Building, the accordion wall was always open between their two softly carpeted, wood-paneled offices. A visitor who telephoned one would often find himself talking to both partners simultaneously.

Whenever there is a lecture date to fill, they both perform on the podium. They share profits equally, sign letters together, seldom use the first person singular when the plural will do.

There is some division of effort, however. Whitaker usually plots long-range strategy, while Baxter devises slogans and labors over pamphlet copy. They both write speeches and hate the job. Before an interviewer, they are each meticulous in pointing out the specific contributions of the other, but neither likes to be upstaged in conversation. When a question is asked, they both leap forward to answer and will interrupt each other frequently.

Clem Whitaker comes naturally by his tone of moral uplift. His father was a Baptist preacher, an uncle a Socialist Baptist preacher. A precocious youngster, Clem covered the California legislature for the Sacramento *Union* at seventeen, became city editor at nineteen. For a period he was a correspondent for the San Francisco *Examiner,* then in 1921 launched the Capitol News Bureau—a political news service for papers around the state which did not have their own Sacramento correspondents. He had worked up to eighty subscribers and was netting twenty-five thousand dollars a year when he sold out to the United Press late in 1929. He had suffered a difficult siege in the hospital and decided that public relations would be an easier way to make a living.

Whitaker ran some minor campaigns (including a vain effort to abolish capital punishment) before he came upon Leone Baxter in 1933. She was a demure widow of twenty-six who had written a little newspaper copy and now had the unlikely job of manager of the Chamber of Commerce of Redding, California.

What brought them together was a referendum over the Central Valley Water Project, an irrigation and flood control development which had been authorized by the legislature. The Pacific Gas and Electric Company, alarmed because the power generated might be sold to public authorities, then forced a referendum. At a meeting of supporters of CVP, Whitaker & Baxter were urged to take on the campaign.

It was a tough fight. Pacific Gas was well heeled, but Whitaker & Baxter were given less than forty thousand dollars, which they would now regard as laughable. They concentrated their energies on the small towns of central California, which would directly benefit from the project, and did a skillful job of getting their propaganda into small-town newspapers. They also made the first extensive use of radio in a state campaign, handling everything themselves—from the production of scripts to sound effects. When the returns were in, the Central Valley Water Project had triumphed by 33,603 votes. Impressed by this performance, Pacific Gas and Electric later put Whitaker & Baxter on an annual retainer. They remain a client to this day.

Clem and Leone were now launched as a partnership, though they did not marry until 1938. Their second year, 1934, established them as a formidable team. Not only did they put over George Hatfield as lieutenant governor, but they had a large hand in defeating old Socialist Upton Sinclair, who was running for governor on the Democratic ticket with a bizarre program to End Poverty in California, which thoroughly alarmed conservative citizens. A quarter-century later, W & B are admittedly embarrassed to talk about the Sinclair campaign. "It was one we hated to handle," said Whitaker. "Sinclair was an old friend of the Whitaker family. It's always difficult to fight a campaign against a man you like personally." Half the Whitakers stopped talking to Clem. W & B took the job, they insist, because they regarded Sinclair's program as a great menace.

Hired for the campaign just two months before election, "We felt we had to do a fast job, we had to make a drastic change in public opinion." Their strategy was the ultimate in what might be called the diversionary technique—shifting attention from Sinclair's program to his personal foibles. In a harsher age, it has become known as the smear job.

"Upton was beaten," Clem says candidly, "because he had written books." For three days, Clem and Leone secluded themselves with Sinclair's lifetime production, compiling a mass of damaging quotations. Then they hired an artist named Bill Le-Noire who did a series of thirty cartoons illustrating "the blot of Sinclairism"—generally a dismaying quotation, embedded in a big blob of black ink, and flung against some typical scene of American felicity.

Thus, bride and groom, emerging from church, are assailed by a Sinclair comment that in capitalist society the institution of marriage has the qualities of "marriage plus prostitution." Or the picture of a madonna and child is defiled by Sinclair's observation that "of a score of religions in the world . . . *each is a mighty fortress of graft.*" In another cartoon, a huge black ogre labeled "Communism" looms behind Sinclair as he harangues a glowing idealization of Miss California. The Communist charge was frequently thrown at Sinclair, though in that regard he was quite blameless.

Whitaker & Baxter had mats made of the cartoons, shipped them to papers around the state. At least three thousand appeared in print. A cascade of pamphlets exploited the same themes. W & B, however, regarded the cartoons as their most effective contribution to the campaign. "Sure, those quotations were irrelevant," says Baxter. "But we had one objective: to keep him from becoming governor. But because he was a good man, we were sorry we had to do it that way."

After their imaginative assault on Sinclair, Whitaker & Baxter found themselves in increasing demand. They have handled as many as six campaigns in a single year. They turned back the repeated assaults of the Single Tax, the $30-every-Thursday movement of the late thirties, the weird pension plans of "Gorgeous" George McClain, the Garrison Revenue Bond Act and an effort to reapportion the legislature. They won an antifeatherbedding drive against the "full crew" law on the railroads, three times persuaded California's voters to raise teachers' salaries, elected one mayor of San Francisco, kept another from being recalled, ran three successful campaigns for Goodwin Knight, one for Earl Warren. They have handled but one Democrat—George Reilly—who was defeated for mayor of San Francisco.

Whitaker & Baxter's "Campaigns, Inc." brought a new approach to political public relations. Long before their advent, politicians and pressure groups had of course hired press agents to write speeches and puff their causes in the papers. W & B, by contrast, provided the entire management of a campaign—overall strategy, organization, financial supervision as well as the mechanics of publicity and advertising.

There was a market for these services because California politics by the early thirties had undergone a strange transformation. The cross-filing system—allowing Republicans and Democrats to run in each other's primaries—had effectively undercut party identity. A mushrooming population, nonpartisan municipal elections, and a dearth of patronage made it impossible to build stable political machines on the traditional model, with organization down to the precinct level. Moreover, incessant use of the initiative and referendum meant that in each election the individual voter had to be continuously harangued about a multitude of complex issues.

Cross filing and the initiative and referendum, ironically, were reforms of the progressive Republican administration of Hiram Johnson. They were designed, in that distant era before World War I, to break the power of the old-line party machines. They achieved their purpose—eventually at the expense of producing chaos in California politics and making politicians more dependent on the mass media than elsewhere in the country. In California, the great game of politics turned into a branch of public relations.

Year-round, Campaigns, Inc.'s office staff numbers no more than twelve people; before election time it is likely to expand to fifty. The firm charges $25,000 to $75,000 to handle a statewide campaign, but this fee is supplemented by the 15 per cent commission charged on advertising placed for clients. (The firm has its own advertising subsidiary.) Annual income is further increased by fees for public relations counseling which occupies the staff between campaigns; clients include railroads, public utilities, steamship lines. Gross income comes to about $250,000 a year—exclusive, of course, of the money expended on behalf of clients. It is not unusual for a statewide referendum campaign to cost $500,000.

The firm's success can be credited to a variety of factors: shrewd strategy, thorough organization and an imaginative exploitation of all the media of communication. By the time one of their campaigns is over, an unwary citizenry has sustained a mass inundation of propaganda. Some years back, Whitaker calculated that in a typical campaign they employed 10,000,000 pamphlets and leaflets; 50,000 letters to "key individuals and officers of organizations"; 70,000 inches of advertising in 700 newspapers; 3,000 spot announcements on 109 radio stations; theater slides and trailers in 160 theaters with a weekly audience of nearly 2,000,000; 1,000 large billboards and 18,000 or 20,000 smaller posters.

Whitaker & Baxter's first step, in taking over a campaign, would be to absent themselves from the office for a few days to work out a detailed Plan of Campaign. This included the basic strategy, methods of organization, the issues to be stressed, the types and volume of publicity and advertising to be used—and the timing of each thrust of propaganda. As a guide to their own strategy, W & B frequently also formulated an Opposition Plan of Campaign.

They also prepared a budget. The client—generally a committee—guaranteed the total sum, and Whitaker & Baxter handled all disbursements, rendering an elaborate account at the end of the campaign. If the treasury ran low, W & B were in a position to advance as much as $100,000 out of their own funds, thus avoiding any slackening in the pace of the campaign because of financial stringencies. Few public relations firms are in this enviable position.

A basic part of the strategy of any campaign is to undercut as much opposition as possible before the propaganda guns are unlimbered. Early in 1958, W & B confronted a difficult problem —how to win a referendum in support of a fifty-million-dollar bond issue to improve the Port of San Francisco. The trouble with this estimable undertaking, they felt, was that only San Francisco would directly benefit, though the voters of the entire state would have to approve. True, the bonds would be repaid out of revenue, and hence would cost the taxpayers nothing— but this was not an easy thought to get across to more than six million voters. "The more you have to explain," Clem Whitaker says sadly, "the more difficult it is to win support."

Their solution was enterprising. One morning at breakfast Leone read a newspaper story about another bond proposal—a ten-million-dollar issue, also self-liquidating, to expand small-boat harbor facilities throughout California. From the look of things, the small-boat bill seemed unlikely to pass the legislature. Whitaker & Baxter had no passion for amateur boating, but they suddenly saw a way of enhancing the attractiveness of their own measure—namely, by amalgamating both bond proposals.

They mobilized their supporters at Sacramento, got a new bill passed, and were then able to go to the state with a proposal to improve scores of harbors from the Oregon border to Mexico. There followed the usual outpouring of catchy handbills, "mailers," newspaper ads, radio and TV spots—and the voters responded handsomely. "A good example," says Whitaker, "of how you can win a campaign in the board room—long before it starts."

The design of campaigns varies, but they share certain basic similarities. Timing is very important. A cardinal W & B rule is to allocate 75 per cent of their budget to the final three or four weeks of a campaign, when the din of contention has finally aroused the voters. They refuse to deviate from this timetable no matter what provocation the opposition offers earlier in the campaign.

Repetition is equally important. "We assume we have to get a voter's attention seven times to make a sale," says Whitaker. "That's an arbitrary figure, of course, but repetition is the only way to swing someone from no position to an affirmative position."

Every campaign must have a dominant, arresting theme. "The theme," Baxter has explained, "should have simplicity and clarity. Most of all, it must high-point the major issues of the campaign with great brevity—in language that paints a picture understandable to people in all circumstances."

Simplicity, of course, can verge on oversimplification and even fantasy. The Truman administration's proposal for compulsory medical insurance was, for better or ill, exactly what the term implied. W & B, however, found it more helpful to crusade against "socialized medicine"—a term which they have conversationally abandoned, now that the fight is won.

In 1950, California's voters were presented with a scheme to pay old age pensions out of the proceeds of legalized gambling. The plan was poorly conceived, but Whitaker & Baxter, who led the opposition, did not confine themselves to attacking its absurdities. Instead they pitched their entire campaign on the theme, "Keep the Crime Syndicates Out!" But nobody had suggested that the crime syndicates be let in.

For each theme, Whitaker & Baxter can of course provide a rationale: compulsory medical insurance would lead to socialized medicine; legalized gambling could lead to corruption. The virtue of a slogan, however, is that it so compresses the sequential relationship that a hypothetical threat readily becomes an immediate threat.

In its printed propaganda—that is, in the small print—W & B will spell out their rationale. Thus, in 1958, their newspaper ads warned that if the Monkey Wrench Tax Bill passed, the state would have to impose new taxes on real estate, food and gasoline in order to raise needed revenues. But their highly effective TV spots eliminated the argument and merely demanded, "Do you want to pay a state property tax on your home?" Loud voice in the background: "NO!" Announcer: "Then vote NO on Proposition 17—the Monkey Wrench Tax Bill." The unwary listener, of course, could hardly have gathered that Proposition 17 was not in itself a real estate tax.

Campaigns are dominated by themes, and themes are in turn highlighted by "gimmicks," a term which W & B themselves apply. The Monkey Wrench Tax Bill was one such attention-getter. So was the song, "I've Been Loafing on the Railroad" when they were campaigning in 1948 against the full-crew law on trains. It was sung at meetings, on innumerable radio spots, and served as caption for a widely distributed cartoon of a railway employee lolling in a bed atop a freight car. That visual gimmick was in turn plastered on billboards up and down the state.

One of their most effective gimmicks, some years back, was a handbill in the form of a cardboard purse and bearing the slogan, "Watch Your Pocketbook." It was widely distributed outside theaters until police suggested it was a menace—for most recipients immediately felt for their wallets, thereby providing invaluable intelligence to any lurking pickpocket.

Contagious themes, arresting gimmicks, a continual drumbeat of radio and TV spots are the only way to arouse the voter from his normal political torpor, in the view of Whitaker & Baxter. "The average American," Whitaker once sadly informed a PR audience, "doesn't want to be educated; he doesn't want to improve his mind; he doesn't even want to work, consciously, at being a good citizen.

"But there are two ways you can interest him in a campaign, and only two that we have ever found successful.

"Most every American loves *contest*. He likes a good hot battle, with no punches pulled. . . . *So you can interest him if you put on a fight!* . . . Then, too, most every American likes to be entertained. He likes the movies; he likes mysteries; he likes fireworks and parades. . . . So if you can't fight, PUT ON A SHOW!"

The show must never lose its aggressive quality—a principle as important as its thematic simplicity. "Even when you're on the defensive, you must appear to be aggressive," says Whitaker. This is not always easy. In 1946, they were campaigning to prevent the recall of Mayor Roger Lapham of San Francisco. A recall campaign, unlike an election, does not involve two or more candidates slugging it out. There is no opponent—just the public official defending his record against his detractors. An intolerable situation, W & B felt; their solution was a brilliant improvisation—Mayor Lapham vs. the Faceless Man, a sinister type with his tilted derby completely obscuring his face, whom they labeled "The Undercover Candidate for Mayor." The Faceless Man, whose non-face was smeared across billboards and newspaper ads, became a target as vicious as any opponent Lapham might have flailed against. Lapham won.

The success of a campaign, W & B believe, is not only dependent on its aggressive pace and streamlined themes. It also requires grass-roots organization for the most effective distribution of the propaganda packaged at headquarters. In each campaign, the firm spends a good deal of energy rounding up its "natural allies"—local and statewide organizations which have either a direct or peripheral interest in the issue at stake.

Thus, in its 1958 campaign for the harbor bond issue, W & B naturally received endorsements from the Pacific American Steamship Association, the various maritime unions, the California Marine Parks and Harbors Association and the California Boating Council. But it ventured much further afield—mobilizing such groups as the California Rifle and Pistol Association, the Associated Brick Manufacturers of Southern California, the Fresno Cotton Exchange, the Chambers of Commerce of over forty cities, and the Orange County Farm Bureau. By the end of the campaign, over 150 organizations had affirmed their approval of Proposition 4. These endorsements served many purposes: before they were obtained, the campaigners had a chance to state their case before a wide assortment of groups; after they were obtained, the co-operating organizations agreed to circularize their memberships with W & B literature; and the endorsements themselves provided the substance for local publicity releases.

Whenever possible, a network of local committees is set up around the state. They take their marching orders from detailed directives from Campaigns, Inc. These list the issues to be stressed in the campaign, the stock replies to be delivered to the charges of the opposition, and the precise methods by which endorsements and publicity can be obtained. For novices, canned speeches are also included.

A concerted effort is made to win the editorial support of newspapers. There is nothing subtle about the approach: the firm's missionaries buttonhole editors in their offices. When they were fighting a compulsory health insurance proposal made by Governor Earl Warren, over 500 newspapers were visited. The results were gratifying: Warren's proposal lost around 30 of its 50 supporters, and the numbers of papers in opposition increased from about 100 to 432.

W & B do not overlook the helpfulness of advertising in encouraging favorable editorial attention. Reporting to its client, the California Teachers' Association, as one of its pay-raise referendum campaigns got under way, W & B stated: "Every newspaper in the State has received a check to cover 60 inches of advertising space, reserved for our use during the month of October. [This was in July.] The individual papers were advised that the schedule was made possible by the teachers in their own communities—and you can feel very confident, I believe, that no editor is going to develop a distaste for teachers generally or for their publicity stories as a result of it."

Further to increase good will, W & B do not charge small papers the normal 15 per cent advertising commission.

In 1948, Whitaker & Baxter first applied their techniques nationally. That year the American Medical Association, alarmed at the Truman administration's campaign for compulsory medical insurance, retained Whitaker & Baxter to turn back the threat. They went to Chicago, recruited a staff of around forty people, spent $4,678,000 over a three-and-a-half-year period.

Their approach was strategically sound: organized medicine had to offer a positive program to counter the administration's plan. Under W & B's prodding, the AMA for the first time enthusiastically backed voluntary group insurance plans, which provided a persuasive slogan—"The Voluntary Way Is The American Way"—with which to belabor "socialized" medicine.

Whitaker & Baxter then set about to mobilize the nation's doctors to arouse their patients, friends and every variety of local organization to the "Socialist" threat. An enormous asset, of course, was the network of county and state medical societies around the country whose members eagerly enlisted in the crusade. Chicago headquarters provided them with canned speeches, canned resolutions, canned press releases for local use. In 1949 over 54,000,000 pieces of literature were distributed, in 1950 over 43,000,000. In one two-week period in October 1950 the AMA spent $1,100,000 in newspaper and radio advertising (more than $2,000,000 was also spent by sponsors of tie-in ads).

No angle was overlooked. The personal physicians of congressmen and senators were approached to solicit their votes. Doctors who knew newspaper editors were asked to request their support. Over ten thousand endorsements of the AMA position were received from local organizations. These were promptly released to the press and brought to the attention of the President, congressmen, senators and state legislators. In the 1950 Congressional campaign, while the AMA officially remained on the sidelines, "Healing Arts Committees" of doctors and dentists were organized to campaign against advocates of the Murray-Wagner-Dingell bill. The "Socialists" were clobbered. So was their bill. Whitaker & Baxter could boast, with pardonable pride, that they had organized the "greatest grass-roots lobby in history."

Success, of course, breeds imitation. There are now several political PR firms in California, some of whose principals—like Herbert Baus of Los Angeles and Harry Lerner of San Francisco—received their training in Whitaker & Baxter's shop. Alumnus Lerner, in 1956, handed W & B their stiffest defeat on an initiative measure to "unitize" California's oil fields and thereby limit oil extraction.

W & B, retained by the "major" oil companies, argued that it was a salutary conservation measure. Lerner, representing the "independents," attacked it as a restrictive measure designed to favor the huge monopolies. W & B's campaign was temperate (friends said they were restrained by their clients), Lerner's attack was slashing—in a fashion reminiscent of his old mentors. His most effective gimmicks, displayed on billboards and ads, were two symbols for the "oil monopoly"—a hog wallowing in oil and a whale swallowing up the independents. His printed copy and TV spots were equally rough—and he won handsomely: 3,950,532 to 1,208,752 votes.

Whitaker & Baxter do not alibi their defeats, but they are of course happier talking about their victories. They have great zest for their work, a quality which they in large part ascribe to conviction. "A campaign is too demanding if your heart isn't in it," says Whitaker. They have never been political neuters, willing to sell their talents to the highest bidder. Republicans from the start, they have regularly worked the conservative side of the street, though certain of their campaigns—like those raising teachers' salaries—had equal appeal for liberal-minded citizens. Dedicated Republicans, they rally spontaneously to any cause which champions Free Enterprise, Personal Initiative, Freedom or the American Way. Their personal rhetoric at times has a quality of Boy Scout piety, but is so insistent that it inevitably carries the ring of sincerity.

Their activities, they insist, have all been to the good. Whitaker is fond of Lincoln's statement, "Public sentiment is everything. With public sentiment, nothing can fail; without it, nothing can succeed."

"If we sometimes go to extremes to create that sentiment," Whitaker has argued, "we can recall that some of the greatest statesmen in American history went to extremes, too. It was Lincoln who said: 'This government cannot endure permanently *half slave and half free*.' That's what we call 'a fear campaign' . . . a picture of dire things to come, unless the issue is resolved.

"And it was Patrick Henry who said, 'Give me liberty or give me death!' That's what we call laying it on with a ladle . . . even in these modern times, that is the kind of dynamic sloganeering that moulds public sentiment—and wins campaigns."

These protestations are hardly persuasive. The sad fact is that their mass manufacture of slogans and wielding of ladles has led to a grievous debasement of political debate. It is true that political appeals, long before W & B entered the scene, were hardly distinguished for their intellectual sobriety. Oversimplification of issues, attribution of base motives to the opposition, appeals to prejudice, and the most irrelevant *ad hominem* arguments have long flavored the rhetoric of democratic debate —especially at election time. Whitaker & Baxter's peculiar contribution, however, has been to make a precise art of oversimplification, to systematize irrational appeals, to merchandise propaganda through a relentless exploitation of every means of mass communication. Compared to these virtuosos, the old-time politician seems like an amateur.

In their more reflective moments, the partners occasionally betray some anxiety about the inadvertent effects of their work. Asked whether they had ever been disturbed at the tactics they have had to employ, Whitaker replied solemnly, "We search our souls to be sure we are not using tactics that will do damage to society." Baxter was more troubled: "We've felt that many of our methods have been used by the most dreadful people—like dictators. The only protection is that people in this business are decent."

The conversation turned again to the 1934 campaign against Upton Sinclair. "We wouldn't operate like that now, would we, Clem?" she said to her husband.

Whitaker sighed. "I guess we've mellowed—but on the other hand, we haven't been faced again with the same kind of fight."

Whatever the character of the fights ahead, their firm can look forward to a secure future. The political atmosphere peculiar to California which first nurtured their talents still exists: the lack of strong party organization, the personal character of many political contests, the enormous number of initiative and referendum issues at every election will continue to provide a ready market for Campaigns, Inc. and its competitors. This despite the fact that the cross-filing system, which frequently nullified the value of party affiliation, has recently been on the way out.

For the last few years, a Democrat or Republican filing in the other's primary had to list his own party label on the ballot, which greatly lessened the chances of capturing both primaries. Then, in 1959, the legislature abolished cross filing entirely. Thus party labels have begun to mean a good deal again in California. All this, however, has not brought into existence strong party organization on the traditional model (despite the growth of unofficial Democratic clubs around the state). Even if they lost political candidates as clients, which seems unlikely, the professional campaign firms could still keep fully occupied with the incessant initiative and referendum campaigns.

Outside of California, the Whitaker & Baxter type of operation has not emerged—nor does it seem likely to. The main reason is that party organization is stronger than in California, even in an era of decline for the big city machine. To hire a PR firm to manage an entire major campaign would involve an unthinkable degree of abdication for a self-respecting political leader. PR people are of course involved in major campaigns in other states. In recent years, they have been put to increasing use and, depending on the prestige of the individual performer, their advice is often taken on issues of policy. But except in isolated instances they are not granted the range of responsibility which W & B take as a matter of course.

On the other hand, the techniques which the California firm pioneered have of course spread throughout the country. The 1952 Presidential campaign—and more particularly the 1956 one —saw a sophisticated effort to merchandise politics with all the gimmickry of advertising and public relations normally applied to the merchandising of soap. We can expect that no future Presidential campaign will be able to dispense with the five-minute TV speech, the thirty-second spot, the canned interview and the carefully scripted political rally, complete to Hollywood director and three name bands. Whitaker & Baxter can reasonably boast that they have led the way.

5

Newsom:

Duplex

Suite

in the

Clouds

The goal of a good many public relations men is someday to attain the lonely eminence of Earl Newsom. His fees are high; his clients include some of the most august names in the corporate roster; and his work involves pure "consultation."

The last is perhaps the most impressive part of Newsom's performance, for in the frenetic world of PR more prestige attaches to living off one's advice than off the product of one's mimeograph machine. Since few practitioners like to be called "press agents," success is often measured in the amount of time one talks to one's clients—and not to the press. Newsom almost never talks to reporters, never sends out a release and only rarely has his staffers undertake anything so prosaic as helping a client run a press conference.

The Newsom operation is fittingly housed in a duplex suite on the thirty-second and thirty-third floors of 597 Madison Avenue—a glowing and softly carpeted expanse of bleached oak furniture and tan drapery. A circular staircase rises gracefully from the reception room to the threshold of Newsom's spacious office. So hushed is the atmosphere that one must strain to detect the tap of a typewriter. In late morning and midafternoon, chic young things noiselessly glide in and out with tea and coffee.

In manner and appearance, Newsom is obviously the type to impress a troubled client. In his early sixties, he is tall and lean, and there is about his craggy and deeply lined face a brooding look of integrity that often suggests a resemblance to Lincoln. It is an impression that is inevitably furthered—through design or not, one hardly knows—by a large print of Honest Abe that adorns one office wall. The impassive countenance of Learned Hand, our greatest living jurist, fixes the visitor from another vantage point and completes, as it were, the psychological setting.

It is doubtless a mark of personal as well as professional security that Newsom is considerably more candid about his operation than many PR men. Ben Sonnenberg, for example, will not furnish a client list or give his fee scale; Edward Bernays will not produce a single name. Newsom, however, immediately rattles off his client roster—Standard Oil (New Jersey), International Paper, R. H. Macy, Campbell Soup, Reynolds Metals, Arthur Young & Company, CBS, Broadcast Music Inc., General Precision Equipment, Eli Lilly and Company, Colonial Williamsburg ("and some of the other activities of the Rockefellers, like Jackson Hole"). For almost thirteen years Newsom also counseled the Ford Motor Company.

The purveying of advice is a lucrative business. Newsom's standard fee is three thousand dollars a month, though he has one account at one thousand and some at four thousand dollars. In addition the client is billed for the services of Newsom's four partners, calculated on a time basis; a charge for overhead is tacked on, plus any out-of-pocket expenses. Newsom's gross (fees and expenses) is something under half a million a year; he will not reveal his profits. The total office personnel, from the six partners down to the receptionist, is twenty-four.

What does he do for his clients? Newsom speaks modestly of his contribution, obviously concerned, as are most PR men, not to embarrass the client by revealing his stage directions. The trade, however, credits him with an outstanding job in designing the public façade of Henry Ford II, who was regarded as a rather inconsequential young man when he took over the Ford Motor Company in September 1945 and who shortly thereafter emerged as an industrial "statesman" of undeniable appeal.

One of Ford's first acts was to retain Newsom; then things started to happen. "Just three events, between the fall of 1945 and the spring of 1946, created the public's impression of Henry Ford," says Newsom. He disclaims, however, any manipulative genius in unveiling the portrait; all his shop did, he insists, was to help "that remarkable young man" display his true face to the public.

The first "event" in November of 1945 was a letter the Ford Motor Company dispatched to the United Automobile Workers. At the time, the long and bitter General Motors strike was on, and labor relations in Detroit was in a generally acrimonious state. The Ford letter, a four-page affair, received all the attentive care from Newsom that he might otherwise lavish, were he a poet, on a sonnet sequence. He is still sufficiently proud of the fourteen-year-old document to keep a copy of it, encased in a leather folder, around his office.

The letter was reasonable and eminently statesmanlike; it argued that since 1941 the Ford company had been the very model of an enlightened employer, only to be victimized by no less than 773 work stoppages. In sum, it asked "the same degree of security as we have given the union itself." The sober, judicious tone of the letter, in the climate of that feverish hour, got it a very good press.

Next came Ford's first public speech, before the Society of Automotive Engineers, in Detroit in January 1946. Because it was Ford's long-heralded debut, the address went through a dozen drafts in Newsom's office and was endlessly revised by Ford and his associates in Detroit. Ford also practiced reading it before his PR advisers; if he stumbled over an unfamiliar word, it would be changed on the spot.

"The Challenge of Human Engineering," when finally delivered, won headlines and long news stories from coast to coast. Flushed with this triumph, Ford next moved to San Francisco, where in February of 1946 he delivered a stirring denunciation of coercive labor legislation and trumpeted that the "one possible solution to our problems . . . is for all of us to pitch in and work." When he finished, the audience of 1,650 in the Commonwealth Club gave him a standing ovation; only President Roosevelt had gotten a bigger turnout. Henry Ford, at twenty-eight, was definitely on his way—and he soon found himself enshrined on the cover of *Time*.

Endowing young Henry Ford with an agreeable face in public was of course a good part of the effort to repair the sagging reputation of the Ford Motor Company. Over the years, the company had declined in public esteem for a variety of reasons for which the elder Ford was responsible—a harsh and capricious labor policy, the anti-Semitism of the Dearborn *Independent*, the old man's isolationist views, his refusal to sign the NRA automobile code in the early 1930's, his incredible *gaffe* in accepting a medal from the Nazi government.

The old image of the company, however, was gradually effaced during the postwar years. The new president emerged as a progressive corporate manager, an enlightened employer, an internationalist, a free trader. He even accepted an assignment as a delegate to the UN. The largesse of the Ford Foundation created considerable good will. Much of the PR effort, of course, was the propaganda of the deed as well as the word—the company's policies did change in important particulars. Newsom hardly deserves sole credit, but through the crucial years he was at young Henry's elbow, prompting him to act in ways which would bring public approbation.

When the task is done and the new image created, each of the steps along the way seems surpassingly easy. Indeed, they were often obvious at the time. The problem, however, is that what is a matter of simple common sense to the PR consultant often seems revolutionary to a businessman accustomed to an unbending attitude toward labor and a stiff reserve in addressing the public. Much of Newsom's success comes from his ability to win the confidence of suspicious businessmen and overcome their apprehensions.

"People give their confidence to Earl very quickly," says W. H. Ferry, a former partner. "They see he's an honest man—the sort to whom they can trust their daughter or their reputation, if they can to anyone. I never saw anybody who could operate so well with people who were jittery. At a board meeting, Earl has a high talent very close to genius in bringing clashing views to some sort of harmony." In the case of the letter to the UAW in 1945, says Ferry, Newsom could have readily won over young Henry to the suggested approach, "but it might have been too quick a victory. There were a lot of mossbacks on the board then, people addicted to the old philosophy of how to handle labor, and Earl felt it was wise to persuade them. So he sat around for three days, with draft after draft of the letter, until he had reconciled all those diverse views."

The shrewd PR man, of course, has a finely attuned sense of when the client should talk and when he should remain silent. Stephen Fitzgerald, another former Newsom partner who is now in business for himself, recalls the perplexity that assailed the Newsom shop in the early months of the Ford account when young Henry received an invitation to appear before a Congressional committee looking into the affairs of the Office of Price Administration. Two days before the scheduled appearance, Newsom, partner Fred Palmer and Fitzgerald sat around until late in the evening discussing the sort of statement Ford should make before the committee. Drafting a plausible statement, however, was not the basic problem. What troubled them was that they could not prepare Ford's responses to the spontaneous questions the committee would throw at him. Their client, they feared, was too inexperienced to handle himself well.

Finally Newsom said, "The solution is obviously not what he'll say, but to arrange that he say nothing at all." Such was his advice. Instead of appearing before the committee, Ford dispatched his views by telegram—suggesting that he saw little point in testifying but that he would be "happy" to if the committee insisted. It didn't insist. "Now, that's what I call a real public relations decision," says Fitzgerald.

Public relations on the discreet and elevated level on which Newsom practices is not something an ambitious young man readily attains. Edwin Earl Newsom served a long apprenticeship. The son of a Methodist preacher, he was born in Iowa, educated at Oberlin. He came to New York in 1923 to study for his Ph.D. at Columbia. His goal was to teach English literature on a college level; to finance his studies, he taught at a prep school in New York. After two years, however, he abandoned the academic life for a job handling advertising promotion on the *Literary Digest*.

This involvement began his long interest in market research studies, opinion sampling and the general problem of how public attitudes are shaped. In 1927, he went to the Oil Heating Institute, as director of advertising and promotion, a job which gave him an opportunity to shape a few public attitudes on his own.

The oil burner industry had quite a problem: multitudes of people, apparently, feared that their homes would blow up if they installed the infernal gadgets in their cellars. "The question was to get over this emotional block," says Newsom, and the solution, in which he had a large hand, involved a number of interesting approaches. The institute offered installation plans to home building outfits around the country; architects were hired to plan playrooms and rathskellers for basements suddenly emancipated from coal dust; photographs of the new model cellar blossomed out in magazines and newspapers.

In two or three years the problem was licked, and Newsom moved on again—to the John Day book-publishing company, where he was a partner; to an investment house, where he handled public relations; to a partnership in the industrial design business with Norman Bel Geddes. His duties involved organization and finances, as well as soliciting new business. It was an exciting operation, but Newsom felt somewhat frustrated. "The problem was that I was a partner in a service firm, but the purpose of the firm was not in my province." In 1935 he left and set up his own PR shop.

From May to October, Newsom and his partner Fred Palmer (who is still with him) did not have a single client. A certain number of straight publicity jobs were offered. "There are always a lot of people who want to be noticed," as Newsom puts it. "I know this sounds stuffy, but I did not want to spend my life doing puff jobs."

In October, on the recommendation of a friend, the first account came—the Atlantic Refining Company, which had just developed what it regarded as a superior lubricating oil. "They all thought it was terribly important, and I thought it was terribly important," says Newsom. "The problem was how to dramatize it for the trade."

The solution was to run a test, using six automobiles which were driven twenty-four hours a day until they each ran 100,000 miles. Newsom publicized the successful results throughout the land. This operation was sheer "product publicity"—an honorable form of salesmanship, from which he has long since graduated.

His second client was the tea industry—on recommendation of a consultant to Atlantic Oil. The tea people were concerned that consumption in the U.S. was far less than in Britain. To discover the cause of this deplorable state of affairs, Newsom had Elmo Roper conduct a survey. Tea, Roper conclusively proved, was regarded by Americans as (a) a sissy drink and (b) a foreign drink. Newsom thereupon devoted himself, for several years, to correcting that impression—deluging all media with information on the glories of tea. This again was product publicity. Tea consumption rose. And tea—again by referral of one of his admirers—led to a similar job with the International Wool Secretariat.

The war years brought Newsom an important corporate

client—the American Locomotive Company. Then, in 1942, came the gilt-edged account which established his status— Standard Oil (N.J.). S.O.J. had a messy problem. The Truman committee was lambasting it for its 1929 agreement with I. G. Farben, which gave the American company access to German patents but which also involved it in an agreement for the division of markets. The cry of cartel and the linkage with the German trust suggested scandalous conduct. S.O.J.'s president, ill-acquainted with the background of the case, made an inept appearance before the Truman committee. To retrieve the company's position, Newsom was hired.

His first move was "to get all the facts" on the Farben agreement and get them out to the public. A long and cleverly written presentation—which argued, among other things, that the German patents were of great help to our war effort—was drawn up for President William Farish, who returned to Washington for another bout of Congressional testimony. He was on the stand for three days, but when he stepped down, Standard was off the hook. His statement was then printed and widely distributed to stockholders and the public.

Newsom's next major contribution was to guide Standard Oil in creating its own PR department—now an elaborate setup headed by Stewart Schackne, a former Newsom partner. "Our technique, you see, is to work ourselves out of a job," says Newsom. Not exactly. S.O.J.'s PR operation handles the daily chores of press relations, community relations, and elaborate good-will projects such as touring the New York Philharmonic in Venezuela and underwriting Robert Flaherty's film about oil exploration, *Louisiana Story*. But Newsom still holds the company's hand and parcels out judicious advice. The same pattern prevails with most of his other clients. For more than a dozen years Newsom has not done any publicity himself.

The beauty of clients like Standard Oil and Ford is that there is never a problem of attracting new clients. The prestige of the patron rubs off on the protégé. Newsom never has to make a "presentation" to a prospect, throw a party to impress him, or even take him to lunch—unless he cares to. Newsom does not even have to name-drop. The PR man who can avoid that indulgence has truly arrived.

He also operates in an area where extravagant claims for the achievements of public relations do not have to be advanced. "Over a long period of time," he is persuaded, "no corporation can be made to look better than it is. The reporting can't be better than the action." This, of course, is the standard patter of the PR counselor, but Newsom adds that "I don't think that you can, by weight of propaganda, change materially people's opinions and attitudes. I think there is incontestable proof that when you wind up to change views which people think are right, you worsen the situation. In the plight Standard of Jersey found itself in, in 1942, it wouldn't have done any good to buy full pages of advertising around the country." These observations, of course, are hardly suggested as an argument against public relations. They are rather an argument against the hard sell. Not all his competitors would agree.

Newsom sees the PR man's role as not only involving policy guidance so that good deeds bring a good press, but also as a kind of suppressor of the bellicose instincts of businessmen. In a speech a few years ago, he said:

"This cadence of statesmanship—as we deal with matters in which public opinion is involved—requires of you and me a certain discipline. We can help our bosses to avoid hasty, hotheaded reply when our institutions are criticized. We can help them to avoid public arguments. A battle of name-calling in the public press does not resolve issues and settle questions—it only creates public uncertainty and distrust of both parties. In this day of tensions—with the fear of the ultimate tension, atomic war, hanging over the heads of all of us—people are puzzled and distrustful *when leaders of institutions serving them seem unable to resolve their differences privately.*" (My italics.)

One need not champion indiscriminate name-calling to doubt whether this muting of controversy serves the public interest. A lack of contention may promote institutional acceptance—the most artful job in PR—but hardly democratic enlightenment.

6

Hill and Knowlton: PR Factory

Decorum is the word for the big-time PR factory. One of the proud boasts of Hill and Knowlton, Inc. is that it never solicits a client. Like a doctor or a lawyer, its shingle is modestly displayed on the thoroughfare, but no effort is made to collar passers-by. Prospecting for clients, one gathers, would be distinctly "unprofessional."

Such restraint, of course, is a luxury which most PR firms cannot afford. Some of them maintain "new business" departments, others pay finder's fees, a few make an elaborate ritual of wining and dining potential clients. Hill and Knowlton can avoid these exertions because it is large and prosperous—one of the "big two" in the industry (the other is Carl Byoir & Associates, Inc.). Its gross billings, according to President Bert Goss, came to $3,500,000 in the fiscal year ending June 30, 1959. (This was exclusive of out-of-pocket expenses charged to clients.) Its profit margin before taxes ranges between 20 and 25 per cent, depending on the year.

Hill and Knowlton's shop has all the discreet opulence and grace of décor of a lushly endowed corporation, with a splendor of wood paneling and luxuriance of carpeting that could hardly be improved upon by its clients. Outside the executive suite, its employees work in subdued, aseptic, air-conditioned comfort; the atmosphere is at the furthest remove from that of a newspaper office.

Staff members are also well paid—from $6,500 for an assistant account executive to $20,000–$25,000 for an account coordinator, who supervises several accounts. They enjoy stability of employment, fringe benefits and profit-sharing—emoluments not commonplace in this volatile industry.

Hill and Knowlton's client list is a roster of corporate distinction—Coca-Cola, Procter & Gamble, Avco, Owens-Illinois, Gillette, Zenith Radio, Royal McBee, Cities Service, among others. It also has a number of trade associations as clients—led by the American Iron and Steel Institute, its biggest account, and including the Tobacco Industry Research Committee, the Licensed Beverage Industries Association, the Newsprint Information Committee (a Canadian group), the California wine industry.

Hill and Knowlton will not reveal all of its clients, who number approximately forty. "We don't give out a complete list because a few are in a confidential status," says Goss. The logic is plausible, though it is always a bit odd when a PR firm refuses to indulge in the candid self-revelation it publicly urges on industry.

Hill and Knowlton did not emerge out of the mists in its present dimensions. Its origin was the one-man operation John W.

Hill launched in Cleveland in 1927, and its story is largely Hill's story, which in turn is a text in the art of pyramiding referrals and thereby edging up the ladder of American business.

Now in his late sixties, John Hill is a stolid, long-faced man who wears rimless glasses and conservative, double-breasted business suits. His manner is grave and low-keyed, with the reserve one associates with bankers; occasionally he will allow himself a ripple of mildly chuckling geniality. He speaks with the measured diction of a man appalled by a lapse in discretion or syntax, yet, like most PR people, he loves to talk.

His early life was both more venturesome and nonconformist than his present demeanor would suggest. He was born on a farm in Shelby County, Indiana, in November 1890, went to high school in Shelbyville, then did a stint on the Shelbyville *Republican* for a salary of six dollars a week, doubling as reporter and advertising solicitor. ("I never sold a nickel's worth of advertising; I was never much of a salesman.")

He enrolled at Indiana University but quit during his sophomore year to return to the family farm and spend a year reading books. "I got Everyman's Library," says Hill, "and decided to read everything from Homer to the moderns; I read about fifteen hours a day. Then I went back to college for another year, but I had learned more at home than I ever did at college."

He again abandoned higher education, worked on papers in Buffalo and Akron. During the summer of 1914, he published a little six-page tabloid called the Chicago *Daily Digest*. It was filled with race results, sporting news and bulletins of more serious import, and was distributed free to hotels and restaurants. Advertising revenue was inadequate, and after a while the printer cut him off.

He then turned to another newspaper job in Akron, where he

made the acquaintance of an enterprising reporter named Ray Sprigle. For reasons that are no longer entirely clear to Hill, they decided to take a canoe trip down the Mississippi to New Orleans. They packed typewriters and planned to write nature stories, but had just begun their journey when family problems called Sprigle back to Akron. Hill then found employment on the Cleveland *News*.

He married in 1916, remained on the *News* until 1917, when he was making twenty-five dollars a week. Dissatisfied over his prospects, he shifted to the Penton Publishing Corporation, working as a financial editor on two of their trade papers. On the side, he launched a weekly business column for the general press, wrote a monthly bank letter for the Cleveland Trust Company.

All this, it turned out, was preparation for a career in public relations. Two factors led Hill to make the switch: he read a speech by Ivy Lee, which greatly impressed him, and he was also dismayed by the quality of corporation news releases which he received as a business journalist. He determined he could do better.

Hill's first client was John Sherwin, chairman of the Union Trust Company in Cleveland. "Sherwin had a fracas coming up in connection with some Goodyear financing," Hill recalls. "He was being opposed by Frank Seiberling, head of Goodyear, who had hired Carl Ackerman to do his publicity. So Sherwin thought he needed someone, and called me in; there seemed to be no one else in Cleveland."

Hill asked for $1,500 a month to do the job; Sherwin offered $500. Hill initially turned him down, then suggested that Sherwin get him some other clients to make up the difference. This was a shrewd move, which was to launch him with the proper clientele from the outset. Sherwin picked up the phone and called E. J. Kulas, president of Otis Steel. "I'm going to send out a young fellow named Hill and I want you to put him on the payroll," he said. It was as simple as that, and in April of 1927 Hill opened his first office—a little cubicle in a communal office, sharing a secretary with eleven others.

Later Sherwin got him some other accounts, but steel was to become his important preoccupation. Cyrus Eaton, already a legendary figure, hired him to do publicity for Central Alloy, which later became a part of Republic Steel. Hill then worked for Republic and became a good friend of Tom Girdler, whom Eaton had imported from Pittsburgh to head the company. The Girdler connection was to become the crucial one.

Early in 1933, when he was grossing $100,000 a year, he acquired Donald Knowlton as a partner. Later that year, the American Iron and Steel Institute decided it needed a public relations director. It was during the NRA days, when steelmen were being called to Washington in droves. Public performance under the flashbulbs, with an irreverent press shooting embarrassing questions, was an unnerving experience for men used to the privacy of their own board rooms. Professional assistance was obviously needed, and Tom Girdler put in a strong sales pitch for Hill. In November he was hired, at a salary of $22,500 a year, with the understanding that he would spend his weekdays working in New York on the steel account, commuting to Cleveland on week ends to look after the rest of his business.

It was the Steel Institute which lifted Hill from the obscurity of a provincial PR operation. As a client, the institute was laden with almost as much prestige as the Rockefeller interests, whose patronage established Ivy Lee as America's foremost corporate apologist twenty years before.

Expansion came gradually, however, and it was not until 1938 that a New York branch office of Hill and Knowlton was established. A few years later, Girdler gave Hill another helpful boost by introducing him to financier Victor Emmanuel, who hired him to represent the Aviation Corporation of America and its subsidiary, Consolidated Vultee. In 1941 Girdler was running the latter firm in San Diego and imported Hill to oversee its public relations.

The first problem was to obtain adequate recognition for Consolidated Vultee's bomber, the Liberator. "It was making sorties in Europe," says Hill, "but the company wasn't getting any credit for it. Every other bomber seemed to be mentioned. So we got together seventeen top newspapermen, chartered a plane and took them out to San Diego to see the Liberator. It was simply an educational trip for them to see what was going on; then we started to get a lot of mentions. There were other public relations problems as well. The company's employment had grown from 5,000 to 100,000 in a matter of months, and there were lots of difficulties communicating with the employees, getting them to understand what we were going to do, there was always one crisis or another."

The war years brought him two other large accounts, as well— the American Shipbuilding Council and the Aeronautical Chamber of Commerce, which later changed its name to the Aircraft Industries Association. Hill was giving progressively less time to his Cleveland operation, and eventually two firms emerged. Hill now retains a small interest in Hill and Knowlton of Cleveland, and Donald Knowlton has a small block of stock in H and K, Inc.

By 1946, the New York firm had seventy employees and a Washington office. Since then, expansion has come at a rapid clip. H and K now employs 210 people and has additional offices in Los Angeles, Chicago, Pittsburgh, Cleveland, Nassau, The Hague, Düsseldorf and Sydney, Australia. It also gives part-time employment to "associates" in several foreign cities.

The large PR factory has nothing in common with the jack-of-all-trades press agent who needs only a mimeograph machine and a telephone to operate. At Hill and Knowlton, every function is categorized, departmentalized and slotted in an elaborate hierarchical tier leading up to President Goss and board chairman Hill.

The headquarters staff is organized vertically and horizontally. Vertical personnel are employees who work on individual accounts—account executives, assistant account executives, writers, secretaries. Horizontal staff, who are not assigned exclusively to any particular account, are grouped in three departments and one "service"; their assistance can be co-opted by any of the account people.

There is an education department—the first such in a PR firm, says H and K—which counsels clients on the variety of ways it can make friends through the schools. The community relations department assists with "open houses," company anniversaries, liaison with city officials and similar matters. The communications service advises clients, in meticulous detail, on how they can spruce up employee publications.

The publicity department handles "press contact" for the entire New York office. Publicity is further divided into general press; women's page; finance and business; TV, radio and movies; magazines and books; and columns, syndicates and wire services.

Hill and Knowlton's fees are in keeping with this dazzling list of services. First comes a retainer of $36,000 a year for corporations and considerably more for trade associations. This token entitles the client to "supervision of the account, counseling by the firm's principals and access to the facilities," as President Bert Goss puts it.

For everybody else on the account—from account executive down to secretary—the client is billed for "time charges." The third item for which he pays is out-of-pocket expenses. Excluding the latter, a client's total fee will range from $36,000 to $250,000 a year, though Goss says that $250,000 is not typical.

In keeping with its austere air of professional restraint, Hill and Knowlton stresses that only a small fraction of its corporate energies is devoted to press agentry. The publicity department in New York has only about fifteen people, including clerks. The firm's definition of publicity is perhaps a bit restrictive, however, being limited to "press contact." Individuals working on specific accounts who prepare speeches, booklets, press kits, question-and-answer folders are not regarded as doing "publicity."

On the other hand, H and K does undertake a number of activities, such as the work of its education department, which would hardly be attempted by a press agent. Does a client firm want to win a bit of kudos by financing a scholarship program, providing research grants or endowing a professional chair? Would it like to run a Business-Industry Education Day, donate some equipment to the local schools, or provide teachers for an occasional class or assembly? The education department, headed by Dr. Albert L. Ayars, suggests just how to go about doing it.

Dr. Ayars helps prepare company case histories for college use and a whole raft of material—booklets, recordings, wall charts, films and film strips—for service in primary and secondary schools.

"A client like Procter & Gamble is an authority on dental

health," Dr. Ayars points out. And so P & G provides instructional material—gratis, of course—on how youngsters should care for their teeth. A sample brochure for the kiddies—entitled "Tom Visits the Dentist"—has some sound advice on "Tooth Builders" (i.e., good food) and tooth-brushing technique, together with a check list for the meticulous. ("Every time you brush your teeth, color the correct square.") The back cover contains a letter to parents, authoritatively suggesting that "Crest With Fluoristan" is the "right toothpaste for your family." Crest, of course, is made by Procter & Gamble.

Client attribution, Dr. Ayars believes, is quite appropriate for instructional material. "My feeling is that every teacher and pupil has the right to know where the material comes from," he says. "On the other hand, it's unfair to advertise in the classroom." Presumably, it is quite reasonable to distribute advertising in the classroom for the kids to take home to their parents.

All this work, of course, involves that oblique courting of good will which large corporations have been persuaded is the soundest method of winning lasting public favor. Such an approach has long characterized Hill and Knowlton's labors for the American Iron and Steel Institute. When John Hill launched the program with one assistant in 1933, the immediate concern was government relations in the first heady months of the New Deal. Since then, the program has vastly expanded; some thirty employees work on the account. Among other things, they produce a quarterly slick paper magazine and a monthly bulletin of facts and figures, issue an elaborate set of educational materials for use at every school level, advise the constituent companies of the institute on how to run their house organs and be well thought of in their communities, and handle an elaborate program of institutional advertising.

Typically, in preparation for negotiations with the steelworkers' union in 1959, the Iron and Steel Institute published
a series of newspaper ads on the dangers of inflation. Because
of the nature of its charter, the institute does not speak for the
industry in labor negotiations; the ads, however, were a preliminary effort to persuade the public of the industry's case. Though
the union was not mentioned, an ad would declare: "75 per cent
or more of the final cost of what you buy goes for labor. . . .
With each round of wage and price increases, your dollars lose
another chunk of purchasing power. If things keep on this way
another twenty years—or ten—or five, what will you get for your
dollar?" One pays for the space, but this, too, is public relations.

Even in meeting crises, Hill and Knowlton tend to take the
long view wherever possible. In the PR fraternity, the firm is
credited with a brilliant inspiration in rescuing the cigarette industry from the most damaging assault it has ever sustained. A
few years ago, cigarette manufacturers had reason to fear a
drastic curtailment of sales as the scientific reports characterizing their product as the cause of lung cancer gained wide circulation. The problem was laid in H and K's lap. Its solution—an
interim one which can well last for years—was the establishment
of the Tobacco Industry Research Committee.

The committee's case was a simple one: there was no con-
clusive proof that cigarettes were the culprit—whatever the
American Cancer Society and other medical authorities thought
—but the industry had an obligation to get the full facts. Without prejudging the outcome, it was prepared to spend a small
fortune in scientific inquiry. A well-qualified and eminently respectable scientific panel was given a free hand to block out the
research and administer the grants; up to January 20, 1959,

$3,200,000 had been appropriated for various studies around the country.

This expensive device has been enough to take the industry off the hook. It can point with pride to its sense of public responsibility, and whenever a new report comes out damning cigarettes, it is able to rush into print with the reminder that the full scientific facts are not yet known. Indeed, Hill and Knowlton are often able to get their client's rejoinder into the same news story with the damaging charges. (Advance release dates on scientific reports make this possible.) All of which, of course, gives the cigarette addict sufficient excuse to continue smoking.

And what if the industry's own scientific research, years hence, should prove that cigarettes are indeed harmful? No problem, one gathers—the client would merely be advised to undertake a well-publicized campaign to eliminate the unhealthy ingredients.

Not every crisis, of course, can be met by a statesmanlike shift in institutional "posture" without recourse to a heavy drumbeat of publicity. When the situation calls for it, Hill and Knowlton can quickly deploy a small army of press agents and blanket every medium of communications. This again is the advantage of the large PR factory.

Such a mass propaganda assault occurs each time a strike approaches in the steel industry. In 1952, there was a bitter, prolonged conflict highlighted by President Truman's taking over of the steel mills, only to be forced to relinquish them by the Supreme Court. In this dramatic encounter, Hill and Knowlton spared no effort in its client's behalf. A staff of over fifty was put on the campaign. Some were shifted from the Steel Institute account, other individuals were co-opted from steel company

PR departments. One group went to work in Washington, others were spotted in Cleveland, Chicago and Pittsburgh; the bulk of the staff worked out of New York. One "team" devoted itself exclusively to speech writing; another handled radio and TV; a third briefed reporters covering the controversy.

H and K's final report detailed a prodigious volume of publicity: thirty-nine booklets, editorial reprints and other matter were distributed to the tune of six million copies; six advertisements appeared in more than two hundred daily newspapers with a combined circulation of some thirty million; the steel companies' case was broadcast in eight TV speeches and four network radio programs; forty other speeches and radio appearances were secured in the Pittsburgh, Chicago, Washington and New York areas. More than a hundred news releases and statements were issued. There was also "preparation of special material for editorial writers, assistance in preparing news and feature stories in *Saturday Evening Post, Life, Collier's, Pathfinder, Time, Nation's Business* and other national periodicals, the preparation and distribution of feature releases to 2,000 women's editors . . ."

Nobody was overlooked, though just what two thousand women's editors made of the strike was not entirely clear.

7

Carl Byoir & Associates:
Third Party
Technicians

There is a refreshing, no-nonsense air about the organization known as Carl Byoir & Associates, Inc., which shares the distinction with Hill and Knowlton of being one of the two largest public relations firms in the country. The top brass at Byoir do not cast themselves in the roles of disinterested social scientists, saviors of the republic or custodians of the corporate soul. Nor do they boast, in the manner of some practitioners, about how much time they spend advising clients on top-level policy and how little on the mundane chores of press agentry.

"We believe in publicity and lots of it," says Gerry Swinehart, chairman of the board. "There is some feeling abroad that a faint stigma attaches to publicity. We have never felt that." Swinehart, a burly, hearty man with a powerful voice, was Byoir's first employee. He has headed the firm since the boss's death in 1957.

For years, Byoir's stock in trade has been its reputation as a hard-hitting, hard-driving publicity outfit that gets results—often dramatic results. For A & P it defeated a tax on chain stores in New York State. For the same client it later overcame the threat of a federal tax proposed by Representative Wright Patman of Texas. For the Tile Council of America it secured many helpful building code changes around the country. For the Eastern Railroad Presidents' Conference it won a veto, in Pennsylvania, of a bill the truckers wanted and the railroads vehemently opposed.

Only in one particular has the Byoir office been unsuccessful —it has inadvertently gotten a great deal of publicity for itself, much of it bad. Byoir's tactics have been highly enterprising, but at times its skillful operatives have been unable to cover their tracks.

The firm has hardly suffered financially from its unflattering press notices. It has about 250 employees and gross billings (apart from out-of-pocket expenses charged to clients) of approximately $3,000,000 a year. Byoir charges an annual retainer of $50,000 for a corporate client—as compared to Hill and Knowlton's $36,000—and $75,000 for a trade association. Its billing system and staff organization are much the same as the rival firm's. In addition to the retainer, which merely entitles the client to the counsel of the top executives, he is charged with the prorated salaries of everybody else who works on the account—account executive, assistant account executive, their secretaries and members of various "horizontal" departments—magazine, radio and television, business and financial, and so forth.

Byoir has twenty-four clients, among them the B. F. Goodrich Company, A & P, American Can, Libbey-Owens Ford, Bendix Aviation, the Hughes Tool Company, Hallmark Cards, Radio Corporation of America, Republic Aviation, I T & T. For a time it represented Foote, Cone & Belding, though why an advertising agency needed a publicity firm was a little difficult to understand.

Carl Byoir, who founded the organization in 1930, had one of the most remarkable careers of any of the pioneers in American public relations. In a crowded room he hardly cut any figure: he was a slight, unassuming man in a brown suit (he invariably wore brown). He lacked the rhetorical flourish of a Bernays, the capacity for self-dramatization of a Sonnenberg. But once he began to talk he was noticed: he had a kind of homespun eloquence about him, an effortless capacity to impress businessmen with the depth of his understanding of their problems. This was his forte; he was one of the great salesmen.

Byoir understood businessmen because he was one. He was no journalist *manqué;* his newspaper apprenticeship had only been a steppingstone to a career in trade. At the age of twelve he had a job filing cuts in the morgue of the Iowa State *Register* in Des Moines; throughout his high school years he worked as a reporter on the paper. By his own account, he was city editor of the Waterloo, Iowa *Times-Tribune* when he was fifteen, managing editor at sixteen. Then he worked his way through the University of Iowa, graduating in 1910. There followed two years at Columbia Law School, where he took his degree in 1912. He never practiced.

During his final year at Columbia, he imported the kindergarten training system of Dr. Maria Montessori from Italy to the United States; Byoir realized $63,000 on the venture. The following year, he and a partner established a children's magazine called *John Martin's Book*, then decided to get into big-time publishing. An advertising salesman's job for the Hearst magazines led, by successive promotions, to the post of circulation manager of *Cosmopolitan*. It was now 1917. Byoir had already established his pattern: to scurry wherever opportunity beckoned, no matter how odd the enterprise. The enterprises were to get even odder.

World War I gave him his first taste of public relations—as a ranking executive of the Committee on Public Information. He handled the distribution of some forty million of the Red, White and Blue Textbooks on our war aims, helped publicize the draft, and was involved in American propaganda abroad. This speciality took him to the Versailles Peace Conference; he also served for a time as publicity adviser to Thomas Masaryk, the first president of Czechoslovakia.

Another public relations chore, in the immediate postwar period, was to help Lithuanian groups in the U.S. in their agitation for an independent homeland. Byoir retained the new Edward Bernays office, at a hundred dollars a week, to write press releases for the campaign.

This was to be Byoir's last PR involvement for a long time. While he was promoting Lithuania, he was also involved in an import-export business with Czechoslovakia. It did well for a time, then lost heavily: Byoir found himself $140,000 in debt. To repay his creditors, as he later told the story, he wangled a lucrative tie-up with a patent medicine firm making a product called Nuxated Iron—an iron tonic which claimed "valuable blood, nerve force, and tissue building properties" due to its ingredients of organic iron and nux vomica. Unhappily, an analysis by the American Medical Association showed that a dollar bottle of Nuxated Iron provided not quite four cents' worth of medicinal iron and only a bit of nux vomica.

Many years later, at a pretrial hearing in the celebrated trucker-railroad litigation (of which more later), Byoir was asked about the unflattering AMA report on Nuxated Iron. "That could be accurate," he replied blandly. "The gross profits in all proprietories and in ethicals are tremendous."

After Nuxated Iron came a variety of nostrums which Byoir promoted with Julius and Louis Tuvin. Among them were Kelpamalt (Byoir maintained he never saw the ad claiming that "Kelpamalt can do the impossible" in putting weight on skinny frames) and Viaderma, a weight-reducing compound to be rubbed on the skin, which the AMA characterized as "humbug." (Byoir said he disagreed with the medical authorities; "the people who used it didn't make any complaints. They paid for it.") Nor had he heard that Kelpamalt, a laxative called Seedol and Kayan were cited by the Food and Drug Administration for both misbranding and adulteration. By this time, his associates were running the business, Byoir claimed; he had other preoccupations, though he remained a stockholder and director of the drug company.

In 1928, ill health took him to Cuba. A new career began: Byoir became a newspaper publisher, acquiring control of two English-language papers, the Havana *Post* and Havana *Evening Telegram*. According to his own account, he soon saw that the only way to increase his papers' revenues was to increase the flow of American tourists to the country. Failing to interest the government's tourist bureau in a publicity campaign, Byoir undertook it on his own, creating the Havana *Post* News Bureau for the purpose. He hired ex-newspaperman Gerry Swinehart at seventy-five dollars a week to head the operation, which was sufficiently successful to impress the Cuban government. Byoir was then taken on at sixty thousand dollars a year. The fee was to pay for everything, including the expenses of a three-room office in New York.

Thus from its debut the Byoir firm showed a rugged insensitivity to the gamy odor of some of its clients. The Cuban government was then in the hands of General Machado, a ruthless dictator who even in that innocent era was a difficult character to beautify for the American public. Byoir's contract, which began in 1931, was to run for five years but it ended abruptly in 1933, when Machado was tossed out by a rebellious populace. Years later, an unrepentant Byoir was to observe, "In many respects I think Mr. Machado was one of the greatest administrators I have ever known. I think he did great things for Cuba, and in the main there were some things I greatly admired and some things that I despised, and that goes for some American Presidents I have known."

The same year that Byoir lost Machado he landed the German Tourist Information Office, an account obtained with the help of George Sylvester Viereck, a well-known Nazi sympathizer. Byoir was a Jew, and there seemed a certain piquancy, widely noted in the trade, in his employment by the Nazis. Gerry Swinehart thinks his old boss was sadly misunderstood: "Byoir always said that at the time he took the contract he did not know what Hitler was planning to do with the Jews"—which would suggest that Byoir was the rare press agent who did not read the newspapers—"but you can be sure that the criticism hurt him personally—as a man, inside."

The man went on to greater triumphs, his façade not badly tarnished, for it was an era in which guilt by association (real or fancied) was a barely known concept. Fortunately, even before his encounter with the Germans, Byoir had acquired a handsome asset in the patronage of Henry L. Doherty, the utilities magnate. Doherty first retained Byoir to publicize his two hotels in Florida and some months later put him in charge of the properties. Doherty kept buying up more hotels, and Byoir found himself running establishments in Miami Beach, Coral Gables, Palm Beach and Nassau and commuting to New York to handle his public relations business.

The Doherty connection provided substantial financial ballast for a fledgling PR operation. It also allowed Byoir to entertain the press more handsomely than other publicity men, which of course helped his other accounts as well. Many press agents could offer an occasional Lucullan debauch at "21" or cocktail extravaganza at the Waldorf. Byoir, however, had the privilege of dispatching friendly journalists for expense-free vacations at the Doherty hotels. Everything was on the house, and one could take one's wife. Some impecunious newsmen even borrowed pocket money from the bartender—and, mercifully, were never dunned for the loans.

Byoir also did a great deal for Doherty—one of his principal services being the kudos he brought him as sponsor of President Roosevelt's Birthday Balls in behalf of the Warm Springs Foundation, an organization which helped infantile paralysis victims. According to Byoir, in 1933 Roosevelt called him in to suggest a campaign for the foundation, then losing a great deal of money. Byoir had the bright idea of "borrowing" the President's birthday—January 30—to run fund-raising affairs in thousands of towns across the country. Roosevelt agreed, and Byoir thereupon drew Doherty into the act, to underwrite the expenses. The balls, which were run for several years, were fabulously successful, Doherty was celebrated as a public-spirited citizen and Byoir's connection with the White House went not exactly unnoticed either. It was to be some years before Byoir emerged as a political conservative, a Taft supporter and later an admirer of Senator Joseph McCarthy.

Throughout the thirties, the Byoir operation was a strange mélange of Florida resort publicity, the President's Birthday Balls (to which Byoir personally devoted two months each year), the embarrassing fling with the Nazi account (eighteen months at six thousand dollars a month) and somewhat soberer undertakings on behalf of a few corporate clients.

In 1936, for example, the Louisiana legislature raised the sulphur "severance tax" from sixty cents to two dollars a ton. The Freeport Sulphur Company quickly retained Byoir to try to reduce the Louisiana rate, fearing that Texas, the other sulphur-producing state, might otherwise increase its tax from $1.03 to two dollars. The public relations problem was starkly simple: Freeport Sulphur was the only company subject to the tax in Louisiana, and the campaign would obviously fail if it seemed merely to be serving a private interest. Moreover, the tax had passed the legislature with but one dissenting vote.

"We planned a campaign," Byoir later recalled, "to show that the tax was not merely against the company but against the interests of the whole economy of the state. It was not merely a publicity campaign. It was a campaign of organizing all of those groups in the state which represented large segments of public opinion; persuading them to take a stand against the tax and permitting us to publicize their positions."

The results were gratifying: the legislature subsequently reduced the tax to Texas' $1.03 a ton and embodied the reduction in a constitutional amendment (subsequently approved by the voters) which afforded Freeport Sulphur the protection that any future tax increase had to be voted by a two-thirds rather than a simple majority of each house of the legislature. It was a dramatic triumph for Byoir, of a sort which inevitably attracted more corporate clients. In 1937, he acquired The Great Atlantic &

Pacific Tea Company, in 1938 Libbey-Owens Ford Glass, in 1940 Schenley. By the early forties the main focus of the firm's work had shifted to corporate public relations and it was well on its way to its present size.

The Byoir organization, like any large PR operation, provides a well-rounded service that includes such relatively undramatic activities as the purveying of financial news, the preparation of annual reports, advice on stockholder, community and employee relations. For some of its clients, Byoir fulfills merely a counseling service, for others it supplements the operation of their own PR departments, and for a third group it constitutes their entire PR operation. Though Byoir's reputation was made as a master manipulator of publicity, the master himself highly prized his own counsel. Years ago, when Byoir established $36,000 a year as a minimal retainer, a new client demanded to know what he received for that handsome sum.

"You get the right to telephone me," Byoir snapped. "If the answer is right, it's worth any sum. If it's wrong, it's worth nothing."

The client thought that reasonable.

In the trade, of course, it has not been the Byoir shop's counsel but its propaganda techniques which have won it the greatest celebrity—as well as a good deal of criticism. Byoir partisans argue that the founder was a public-spirited citizen, who always favored "educational campaigns" over crude lobbying. As one Byoir alumnus put it, "Sure, you could buy off a couple of state legislators and stop a bill in committee. But what would happen next year? The opposition might lay two G's more on the line and you'd find you had lost out. Carl always maintained that it was far better to arouse the public to the justice of your cause and have them apply pressure on the legislature. That way a case stayed sold." And that way, as well, a public relations man could justify his employment.

In its disinterested efforts at public enlightenment, the Byoir organization has become indissolubly linked with a PR gambit known as the "third party technique." Byoir did not invent it, but he carried it to a high point of perfection. Briefly put, the technique involves getting some presumably disinterested third party to "front" for your client in a controversy. If the client is trying to push a bill through the legislature, his own eloquence may get him scant attention, but if a wide assortment of farm, business, professional and women's groups all join the crusade, editors and legislators may well be impressed by the apparent ground swell of support.

There are times, of course, when the support is genuine and the third party has a real or felt coincidence of interest with the principal. But when this is not the case, how does one attain such impressive backing? In two ways—by influencing the leaders of complacent groups and by forming new "fronts." The Byoir office has excelled in both methods.

Its virtuosity was first on display in the defensive action it mounted for the A & P, in the late thirties, against taxes on chain stores. After it defeated a proposed New York state tax in 1938, Byoir embarked on a national campaign against the far more serious threat posed by federal legislation. Byoir and the A & P created—and paid the bills for—such presumably independent outfits as the National Consumers' Tax Commission, the Emergency Consumers' Tax Council and the Business Property Owners, Inc. This last group, headed by one Oscar E. Dooly, Jr., who was on Byoir's payroll, was so well camouflaged that not even the A & P's own field staff knew the true story.

The federal tax sponsored by Representative Patman died in

committee after a six-week hearing in 1940. "From that time until today," Byoir boasted in 1949, "we have opposed 247 anti-chain store bills, introduced in state legislatures. Only six passed. . . . In the past eight years not a single anti-chain bill has become law."

There was an embarrassing sequel to Byoir's A & P connection. In 1946, when a federal court in Danville, Illinois, convicted A & P of conspiracy to violate the Antitrust Act, Byoir was included among the culprits. A & P was fined $175,000, Byoir $5,000. The decision was reaffirmed by the Seventh Circuit Court of Appeals and was not appealed to the Supreme Court.

In recent years, Byoir's main achievement in the birth and nurture of fronts was revealed in the celebrated legal brawl between the truckers and the railroads. In October 1957, in the U.S. District Court for the Eastern District of Pennsylvania, the Byoir firm was found to have been engaged in a conspiracy to violate the antitrust laws, together with twenty-six eastern railroads, and the Eastern Railroad Presidents' Conference, its client. The basis for the judge's decision was the devastating public relations and lobbying campaign which the defendants had conducted against the truckers in several states.

The agitation against the truckers, Federal Judge Thomas J. Clary held, involved "a conspiracy in unreasonable restraint of trade, the nature and purpose of which was to injure the truckers in their competitive position in the long-haul freight industry in the northeastern section of the United States . . . as a result of this campaign [the truckers] were categorized as law-breakers, road-hoggers, completely indifferent to the safety of others on the highway and moochers on the public through failure to pay their way."

For their part the defendants argued that they were only ex-

ercising their rights of petition and free speech, that their allega-
tions against the truckers were true, and that the trucking industry was in itself in restraint of trade. At the present writing,
the defendants have an appeal under way, but the facts about
the Byoir firm's activities are not in any substantial dispute.

At the outset of the PR campaign in 1949, Reynolds Girdler,
then account executive, wrote an interoffice memorandum which
succinctly set forth objectives and methods: "For our purposes,
any story, radio program, picture or project on the general
subject of national transportation which would dramatize the
crowded highways, the damages being inflicted on the highways
by heavy trucks and the heavy costs such roads are imposing on
the citizen as distinct from the trucker, would be welcome." All
Byoir departments were to be mobilized.

Reynolds pointed out that the effectiveness of the campaign
depended on keeping the railroads in the background. Staff
members should be guarded if asked about the nature of their
work. He emphasized that "this account is utterly unlike the
conventional one. Here we do not have a client for attribution.
Of course, we will release some stories under client attribution,
but they will be of lesser propaganda importance than those we
can generate from motorists, property owners, taxpayer, farmer
or women's groups. In sum, we not only have to create publicity
ideas; we also have to go out in the field and create the groups
and occasions so that those publicity ideas will become realities."

Out in the field, Byoir's minions generated groups and occasions with great enthusiasm. A more elaborate panoply of
fronts—both existing groups and new "paper" organizations—
would be hard to imagine. A Byoir staffer took over the good
name and office space of the Pennsylvania Grange for a stream

of anti-truck propaganda. The Pennsylvania State Association of Township Supervisors was also very co-operative.

In New York, women's groups were rallied by Mrs. Bessie Q. Mott, a veteran professional clubwoman and Byoir retainer, whose base for the anti-truck campaign was the New York State Federation of Women's Clubs. Years before, she had performed similar services for the A & P.

The New Jersey Automobile Owners, Inc., founded in 1938, was reactivated, with the generous assistance of a Byoir functionary, to carry on the good fight. (The logic, of course, was that automobile owners objected to trucks.) This same Byoir operator was also most helpful in establishing the New Jersey Citizens Tax Study Foundation. Byoir's client paid bills for both groups. A Byoir memorandum informed staff members: "We are also assisting in the formation of a new group: New Jersey Citizens Tax Study Foundation . . . ALL LITERATURE, ETC from this group must be on plain paper, and mailed from NJ."

To enlighten the citizenry of New York about the evils of trucks, another Byoir staff man set up the Empire State Transport League. "A strictly paper organization," Judge Clary called it in his decision, "with its principal office at a desk in a public stenographer's office in Albany, N.Y. Byoir induced many prominent New Yorkers to lend their names. . . . The amount of anti-truck literature and news releases critical of the truckers put out by this organization was prodigious. Of course, it was all at the expense of the railroads without any attribution of responsibility to the railroads."

Byoir had died many months before the court decision, but his protégé, Gerry Swinehart, brushes aside criticism of the firm's front operations. "Hell, it's done all the time in politics. I think it's part of the group motivation and psychology in the United

States. To my dying day, I will maintain that we didn't do anything illegal or unsavory." Moreover, he would not call something like the Empire State Transport League a front. "The men
in the group were shippers and we went to them openly," says
Swinehart. "Our people represented themselves as from the
Byoir organization."

Only their audience was deceived.

The formation of fronts was not the whole of the Byoir operation, of course. Every medium of communication was essayed to
disparage the truckers. The approach was often circuitous and
usually imaginative. The flavor of the radio and TV program
can be gathered from a memorandum, written by Chan Hadlock
in 1952, which spoke of "the desire of the account to utilize
existing radio and television vehicles to portray truckers as evil,
sinister wrong-doers."

Basically this involved attempts to persuade radio and TV
writers to portray truckers as "heavies" as well as an effort to
sell free-lance scripts "with the trucking theme as basic plot,
picturing the trucker as a law-breaker etc." This had to be
handled with some subtlety: "As we discussed, invariably to
conform with network requirements the 'bad' truckers may have
to be compensated for by 'good' truckers, but the poison will
still be there and the damage done."

The Byoir office also distinguished itself for the volume of
anti-truck material it managed to get into national magazines.
It was a storehouse of research data for writers with assignments
in the field and it also proposed possible articles to editors or
free-lance writers. Byoir officials maintain that they only paid
writers' expenses, on occasion, and never any fees, hence offering
no conflict-of-interest to the writer's responsibility to his magazine. There is on record one instance, however, in which the

then head of the magazine department, Patricia Lochridge Hartwell, seems to have played a rather creative role in the development of an article.

Judge Clary, in his opinion, described the incident: "An article which represented an extremely important item in the railroads' campaign against the truckers was that which appeared in the April, 1952 issue of the *Country Gentleman*. This article by Emilie Hall, described as 'You Can Have Better Roads' was referred to by the magazine as a 'new chapter in the farm roads story.' The writer was discovered by Horace Lyon, a Byoir employee assigned to the ERPC account, and Mrs. Hartwell did most of the research and editing for the article, with Jim Miller and Dick Strouse of Byoir helping in some last minute rewrites. Quoting Mrs. Hartwell's appraisal of the publication of this article: 'This was a difficult job to put across, entailing two complete rewrites of the article to satisfy both a pixie author and a difficult editor. This was accomplished without too much pain and the underlying philosophy of the ERPC account came through in the final draft.'"

Byoir executives have reason to be relaxed at the criticism directed at their handling of the railroad account. In the five years after the court proceedings began in 1953, Byoir & Associates gained six new clients. Their admirers did not overlook the fact that in the Pennsylvania engagement which precipitated the court battle Byoir reached its objective: in 1951 Governor Fine vetoed a bill raising the loads which trucks could carry on the highways. That bill had been the focus of the activity in Pennsylvania.

"We have been flattered since the trial," says Gerry Swinehart, "by frequently hearing it said that 'here are people who accomplish what they set out to do.'"

On the other hand, one consequence of the well-publicized litigation was that in 1955 a similar bill of benefit to the truckers was passed by the Pennsylvania legislature *and* signed by the governor.

The moral, apparently, is that a PR firm should keep its name out of the headlines.

8

The Quick
Stake

Two of New York's newer PR operations—Ruder & Finn, Inc. and Edward Gottlieb & Associates, Ltd.—are models to fledgling press agents of the speed with which young men of abundant energy, sprightly imagination and no cash can build a profitable stake in this buoyant industry.

William Ruder and David Finn set up their first office in what is now the linen closet of the Lombardy Hotel, back in 1948. Today they have about 120 employees, two floors of a building on East 59th Street and a volume of business that in 1958 reached $1,800,000 (of which an estimated 80 per cent represented fees). They also operate a Field Network throughout the U.S., have similar part-time representatives throughout the world.

Ed Gottlieb began his independent career, late in 1947, with some sublet space in a midtown lawyer's office. Today he does a volume of approximately $750,000 (fees and expenses), employs 40 people, has offices in New York, Los Angeles, Washington and Paris and takes home $40,000 a year. His New York headquarters, a slickly furnished suite, formerly housed the editorial offices of the defunct *Collier's*—a fitting symbol of the rise of public relations while the media decline.

Both Ruder & Finn and Gottlieb first made their success in the area known as "product publicity"—hymning the glories of consumer goods in much the same fashion as entertainment press agents celebrate "personalities." It is a form of PR which has the advantage of being directly tied in with sales. Results can be proven more readily than if the assignment is, say, to renovate a corporate reputation. The only difficulty is that the PR man must share credit with the advertising agency.

Ed Gottlieb, now forty-nine, came to public relations after several years as a newspaperman. A University of Wisconsin graduate in the depression year of 1932, he was forced by lack of funds to abandon his ambition to go to medical school, instead took a job as office boy at the old Universal Service, a Hearst news agency. After three months he began to write science stories, soon had a by-lined column on science and a salary of fifteen dollars a week, later raised to twenty-five dollars. He eventually became a general assignment reporter, worked for Universal in London and Berlin, then switched to International News Service.

By 1940 he was making seventy-five dollars a week and had the job of night editor for INS in New York when the Carl Byoir office offered him ninety dollars a week. Gottlieb's motives in crossing the great divide were hardly novel: "I didn't have any strong ideals or illusions about public relations, but I was going to make more money. I also had gotten married and I was fascinated by the hours—9 to 5. At INS, I had been closing the night wire at 1 A.M."

Gottlieb flourished at Byoir's, serving at different times as an account executive, chief of the magazine department and head of the radio department. In 1947 the opportunity dreamed of by all ambitious PR men suddenly accosted him: a client who was willing to retain him personally at twenty-five thousand dollars a year. With so dazzling a fee, he could afford to go into business for himself. He pledged his exclusive services for a year and started to boom Toni home permanents.

A rhapsodical glow breaks over Gottlieb when he talks of that first venture. "The publicity and public relations job for Toni was outstanding. I had articles in *Reader's Digest, Life*, practically every woman's magazine, not necessarily mentioning Toni, but saying that beauty shops charge you ten dollars and you can do the same job at home for a dollar or so." His client would necessarily benefit from such suggestions, even if its brand name was left out.

"The slogan, 'Which Twin Has The Toni?' caught on beautifully. We had seven or eight sets of twins and put on displays, with the twins performing, at Macy's, Gimbels and stores across the country. We got a major piece in the *Saturday Evening Post* on how the twins were selected. All I had to do was suggest it— it made great art and was a damn good story."

At the same time, of course, Toni went in for extensive national advertising. Sales boomed. When the owners of Toni finally sold out to another company for twenty million dollars, Gottlieb shared in the glory—if not in the money.

His next big job was for the Block Drug Company, publicizing a toothpaste called Am-i-dent. Its PR virtue, as Gottlieb saw it, was the assertion that it controlled caries. In a six-month period, he managed to get articles dealing with the medical claims of Am-i-dent into *Better Homes & Gardens, Reader's Digest, Time,* and other journals. Without benefit of advertising, Am-i-dent sales, previously minuscule, increased to the point where three factories were required to satisfy the demand. "I was beginning to make a reputation," says Gottlieb.

He also made a big splash in the foreign field. In 1949 a friend in a London advertising agency recommended him to the Dutch bulb industry, which wanted to push its sales in this country. Gottlieb pushed with vigor. Then the cognac industry of France, whose product for years had been curiously neglected by American drinkers, asked him to compete with five other companies for their account. Gottlieb competed and won.

As mentioned earlier, Bill Kaduson, an irrepressible, fast-talking former United Press editor, was put in charge of the account a few months after it began. "Our job," he says, "was to get the American people acquainted with cognac—literally to resurrect the word." The resurrection involved many things. Press releases regularly went out to food editors, offering guidance on how to drink cognac, cook with cognac, flame cognac or serve it at a party. A professional gourmet named James Beard was hired to pretest recipes before they were showered over the hinterland. He also presided over a series of "cognac and coffee" tastings which Kaduson persuaded leading hotels and restaurants around the country to hold.

Wherever a rustle of attention—and perhaps a newspaper plug —might be secured, Kaduson handed out generous samples of his client's product. Free cognac was distributed at the opening of a new play by Jean Anouilh, at an International Trade Fair, at the annual dinner of the Travel Writers Association. "We gave the stuff away in hospital charity wards on New Year's

Eve, on ship cruises, store openings, bar mitzvahs," says Kaduson. "Every Christmas we handed out miniature bottles to Santa Clauses shivering on the street—on condition that they drink the stuff while working."

There were all manner of stunts, such as persuading that well-known milk lover, Premier Mendes-France, to show himself drinking cognac and champagne when he visited the U.S. in 1954. "We knew what the political pressures on him were, so it was not very difficult to obtain his co-operation," says Gottlieb. Equally memorable was the appearance of James Beard on the Jack Paar television show to prepare "the world's biggest crepe suzette"—an immense pancake six feet in diameter. Beard sprinkled cognac over it from a gallon bottle, applied a blowtorch to flame it.

No angle was overlooked: Kaduson even had some solemn research prepared on the "nutritional and therapeutic aspects" of wine and cognac. And results were spectacular. Cognac sales in the United States increased from 150,000 cases in 1951–52 to about 400,000 cases in 1957 (there was then a decline of some 40,000 cases in the recession year of 1958). Advertising appropriations had also been increased, of course. "I've never claimed full credit," says Gottlieb, "but we certainly played an important role." Sufficiently important, at any event, for the cognac people to go on paying him $125,000 a year (a sum which includes expenses), and for the French glove industry and Paris' *haute couturiers* later to retain his services.

Like the entertainment press agent who tries to work his way up to product publicity, the product publicist yearns for the heightened prestige that goes with "counseling" a corporation on the full range of its PR problems. "It takes time," says Gottlieb. "You don't become a counselor until you are respected." But it is a status jump worth trying, not only for prestige but for the security of one's accounts. "I learned in the Byoir organization," says Gottlieb, "that the more ways you can be of service, over and beyond what you're hired for, the more likelihood is there of a long association."

He assiduously applied this lesson in cultivating the Chesebrough Company (now Chesebrough-Pond), which first entered his life in 1951. Gottlieb had made a speech before a trade association detailing some of his publicity coups; a vice-president of Chesebrough was fortunately in the audience and a month or so later he telephoned with a problem. Chesebrough was having trouble marketing a product known as Vaseline Sterile Petrolatum Gauze, which is used in the treatment of burns.

"The difficulty," Gottlieb recalls, "was that doctors were being convinced that dry dressings were better for burns than wet ones. A lot of medical papers had appeared, and also an article in the *Saturday Evening Post*. I knew that in order to persuade the medical profession a good deal of money would have to be put up to finance research or to find out what was already being researched in the field and to hasten its publication. I took my courage in my hands and told them that it would probably cost as much to hire us for all their publicity work as for this particular product." He prepared a memo outlining a program for burn dressings as well as a publicity effort for Chesebrough's other products and suggesting a budget of $45,000, of which $24,000 would be his fee. It was accepted.

Fortunately, Gottlieb found that there was already a good deal of medical research in favor of wet dressings, though he later persuaded the client to finance additional research. A full-scale publicity effort was immediately launched. The well-known science writer, J. D. Ratcliff, was hired to write a pamphlet called "What You Should Know About Burns" for mass distribution to insurance companies, industrial plants, fire departments, and other presumably interested parties. A special pitch was made to the women's magazines. Films came in for attention. Reporting one coup to his client, Gottlieb's office noted that "Through our work, the new Red Cross film awaiting Washington approval pictures a large jar of Petroleum Jelly in connection with burn treatment."

A major effort was directed to persuading state Civil Defense of the merits of wet dressings. The method was to get them to adopt as their "official emergency treatment guide" a recent medical pamphlet on atomic bomb injuries which, among other things, plugged Vaseline Sterile Petrolatum Gauze. Gottlieb's client, of course, was not so much concerned with the sale of its product in the event of atomic air raids as with the harmful propaganda effect of Civil Defense's prevailing preference for dry dressings. In September 1951, for example, forty-one state Civil Defense organizations were recommending dry dressings. By March 15, 1952, as the result of several months' effort by the Gottlieb organization, the box score stood at thirty-four state organizations and the District of Columbia recommending the petroleum gauze.

While these propaganda efforts were going forward, an energetic product publicity campaign was also carried on in behalf of such other Chesebrough products as Vaseline hair tonics and "Lip Ice." After his first six months on the account, Gottlieb managed to make himself even more helpful by launching a program to protect the Vaseline trade-mark, advising on the Chesebrough annual report and recommending an elaborate program of employee public relations. In 1953, he launched the company house organ, the *Chesebrough World,* in 1954 began to produce the annual report, in 1955 arranged the publicity for the merger with the Pond Company and the seventy-fifth anniversary celebration of the firm. By 1957, Gottlieb was operating with a budget (fees and expenses) "in the vicinity" of $125,000 a year. The following year he also found time to handle a couple of plant closings—always a touchy PR problem—and to help fend off the teamsters' union, which was seeking to win a National Labor Relations Board representational election at the firm's Clinton, Connecticut, plant.

The antiunion campaign, on which the Gottlieb office worked with Chesebrough-Pond's managers, was the sort of low-keyed but nonetheless effective effort typical of an era in which the subtleties of public relations have replaced more muscular forms of persuasion. As Gottlieb's report phrased it, the campaign was designed to prove, to no one's great surprise, that "The company was not 'anti-union' but believed a union in this situation would not serve the best interests of the employees themselves." The particular teamsters' local concerned "had a reputation of being honest" but it was part and parcel of the unprepossessing teamsters' international "and therefore the company was opposed specifically to this union."

To communicate its point of view the company held two plant meetings and sent a series of seven carefully worded letters to each employee. As Gottlieb's report later put it: "Recognizing the need for good relations with the union agents should the union win, we divided our letter campaign into two parts. One consisted of letters signed by Tony Oladko (who was vice-president in charge of domestic manufacturing), written in a warm, friendly, sincere, low-pressure key, which outlined in detail, employee benefits, fringe benefits, company plans, employee grievances, job security, working conditions, and wages. The

second set of letters, signed by Jay Calvert as Director of Personnel, were cold, factual letters which linked the Local 443 to the
Teamsters International Union, and which were attached to a
series of reprints from the *Reader's Digest, U.S. News & World
Report* and *Newsweek*, all relating to corruption in unions with
special emphasis on the Teamsters."

In the end, the employees voted down the union. To ward
off any future threat, Gottlieb advised his client to undertake
more extensive "communications" with its workers and perhaps
set up "some form of employee representation council"—in less
circumspect language, a company union. In seven years with
Chesebrough, Gottlieb had come a long way from product
publicity.

Bill Ruder and Dave Finn made their debut in public relations
on a much more modest scale than Gottlieb. Friends since child-
hood when they had gone to Hebrew school together, they both
graduated from the College of the City of New York in 1942.
Ruder later held a job in Sam Goldwyn's publicity office; Finn,
an aspiring painter, was completely innocent of press agentry.
Their ambition, by the time they were twenty-six, was to have
a business of their own; just what business was not too important.

Their first notion, on which they lavished a handsome presentation book, was a merchandising project called "Art in Industry." It was an imaginative undertaking, which unfortunately
attracted no clients. Then an acquaintance suggested they do a
product publicity job for Perry Como's records. The fee was a
hundred dollars a week. In quick order they added three other
small accounts for another hundred dollars and were able to
finance an office and a secretary.

"For Perry Como," says Finn, "we felt it important to get a

continuous showcase. We probably went to 1,000 disc jockeys and offered tapes with Perry saying a few words, to be interspersed between the records. We wound up with 250 or so stations around the country presenting Perry Como shows. At the end of the first year, *Billboard's* poll of disc jockeys voted Perry the most cooperative recording artist. We worked for him for four or five years and got up to $200 a week. We also did some work for Dinah Shore, Burl Ives, the Mills Brothers.

"Our first non-entertainment client came from an item we read in *Retailing Daily* about some fellow with a plastic doughnut-making machine. They had a demonstration girl in the basement of Macy's, but business wasn't so hot. After we were retained, we got a story into one of the papers and they started doing a land-office business in Macy's basement. The next door exhibit was a coffee machine—called a Tricolator. The exhibitor was so impressed with the job we did for the doughnut maker that he got in touch with us." In one of the oddest reversals of PR form, the client eventually wound up as an employee of Ruder & Finn.

In 1949, they established their "Field Network"—"stringers," paid on a per-job basis, who could mount local publicity campaigns. The network was an attractive selling point. A major soap company was one of the first to retain its services and Ruder & Finn covered themselves with sudsy glory. By 1950 they had fourteen people working in two rooms.

Their gross billing was $150,000 in 1951, $470,000 in 1953, $900,000 in 1955, nearly $1,400,000 in 1957. They became noted in the business for aggressive salesmanship ("We've been criticized for soliciting clients," says Bill Ruder, with a shrug), a multitude of clients and rapid client turnover—a sore point. True enough in the past, says Finn, but for the last three years the client list has been more stable.

Their fees range from $24,000 to $48,000 a year, with one client paying $50,000 a year. These are total fees, with no "time charges" added on; they are respectable figures, though some distance from what Hill and Knowlton and Carl Byoir would charge. Their regular client list consists of forty-eight accounts, of which International General Electric, Allied Chemical, Union Carbide, Johnson & Johnson, Bissell Carpet Sweeper and the Hotel Corporation of America are perhaps best known.

Most of Ruder & Finn's efforts, however, have been on behalf of little-known companies eager to increase their sales, win a measure of public recognition or, preferably, do both. Typical was its campaign for Miniature Precision Bearings, Inc., a modest Keene, New Hampshire, enterprise which turns out ball bearings.

Offhand, the problem of creating—let alone projecting—the corporate image of a ball-bearing manufacturer would seem to be a formidable one. The product was certainly lacking in glamour, and the firm was small, with a gross of only $3,500,000 when Ruder & Finn took over the account in 1957. On closer examination, MPB had one decided advantage: its ball bearings, used in instruments and small mechanical devices, were tiny. The whole day's production of several hundred workers could be held in two hands; its smallest ball bearing, as Ruder & Finn is fond of pointing out, was no bigger than the period at the end of this sentence. Miniaturization was indeed an exploitable gimmick.

The PR campaign had as its objectives to acquaint wide reaches of industry with the wonders of miniaturization, to puff MPB's technical and managerial proficiency and generally to make the company better known "to all publics." Ruder & Finn went forward on each front simultaneously. One of its targets was the technical and business press, which can hardly fill its pages without the eager collaboration of PR firms. In 1957 and 1958, articles appeared in *Iron Age*, the *Journal of Commerce*, *Dun's Review*, *Electronics*, and *Steel*, among others. *Fortune*—a high prestige item in any PR clip book—also devoted some attention to the company, and the New York *Times Sunday Magazine* ran a picture story.

Meantime, Ruder & Finn designed a new MPB logotype (the old one seemed too stodgy), prepared a handsome annual report, and devoted itself to such arduous efforts as finding a slogan for MPB's Split Ball Bearing Division. "We convened a series of creative meetings on the subject—you know, brainstorming sessions," says vice-president Norman Weissman. "It's standard procedure around here." The brainstormers produced such inspirations as "Compressed Power in a Standard Bearing" and "Super Strength in a Standard Bearing."

The major effort to put MPB on the map, however, was its award program. Many industrial awards, says Weissman, are too blatantly commercial—the contest somehow involves usage of the product of the company donating the award. MPB, by contrast, was persuaded to pitch its effort on a high plane—providing an annual award to the individual or organization "judged to have done the most to further the concept of miniaturization," regardless of whether that individual or organization fancied miniature ball bearings.

The great virtue of an award is that it casts the donor in the role of public benefactor, it can elicit a good deal of publicity and be held down to a moderate cost. The budget for MPB's first award, conferred in 1958, was a mere six thousand dollars.

From the outset, the program was carefully stage-managed so that maximum publicity could be achieved at each step from the initial announcement of the award to the final selection of the winner. Early in October 1957, a cocktail press conference was held in New York to announce the award to the trade press. A flurry of stories followed. Then MPB sent out twenty-five thousand copies of the award brochure, setting forth the details of the contest, to its customers, research groups, government departments. "That gave a lot of exposure," says Weissman. For a month thereafter, MPB devoted its regular advertising program in the trade press to celebrating the Miniaturization Award. More exposure. Further promotion followed in MPB's house organs, one of which reaches twenty-five thousand engineers.

All this effort brought forth 54 entries—a respectable figure. When the winner was selected—an electronic subassembly, which did not use ball bearings—nothing less than an Award Dinner at the Waldorf-Astoria was appropriate to trumpet the news to an expectant public. A total of 115 guests, including 15 "key trade editors," attended. Horace D. Gilbert, MPB's president, was toastmaster, and Dr. Allen V. Astin, director of the National Bureau of Standards, was on hand as main speaker. The festivities naturally prompted additional publicity, largely in the business and trade press. Further coups followed: pieces in *The New Yorker* and the New York *Times* and a United Press International interview with Gilbert which reached papers throughout the country. MPB was so pleased with what a mere six thousand dollars had bought that the following year it raised the award budget to ten thousand dollars.

One of Ruder & Finn's main preoccupations has been to create a readily identifiable corporate image of its own. Diligent inquiry indicates that it is the only PR firm which puts out an annual report, giving its gross billings and client list. The 1956 report also included profit figures—which were meaningless, however, inasmuch as the owners did not indicate how much they drew individually.

Ruder & Finn also take their responsibilities as citizens quite seriously, devoting 10 per cent of their corporate energies to nonprofit work. In this category of clients are the Hillside Hospital and the Jewish Theological Seminary, a connection they attained through Dave Finn's uncle, Dr. Louis Finkelstein, who is head of the seminary.

They are earnest and somewhat boyish young men, concerned with a variety of matters over which most PR men do not trouble themselves. The partners, for example, called in a management counseling firm when they became hopelessly entangled in intricate office procedures of their own devising. They then got disentangled and completely revised their table of organization.

They have a passion for staff meetings and for lengthy documents codifying the principles and procedures of their business. Back in 1957, after several months of discussion by both their executive and operations committees, they issued a report on "Ruder & Finn Goals" in order, as they explained, "to help us be as constructive as possible in our self-appraisal as a company" and also to help in conversations with client prospects. The first R & F goal, under the heading "General," was "To conduct our business within the framework of human dignity and decency."

These solemnities aside, the partners proceeded in highly dignified fashion to their financial objectives, among them "To maintain a healthy business, with the greatest possible long-term security for the enterprise" and "To provide a good, but circumspect, income for the owners of the business." There were also

"Operational" goals, among them such commendable desires as "To do work for our clients which has an economic value commensurate with their payments to us" and such practical considerations as "To work for clients who are good credit risks." Nor were "Social" goals neglected, it being the purpose of Ruder & Finn, other distractions notwithstanding, "To develop the nature of our work so that it can perform the highest degree of public good, thereby providing a work outlet that will appeal to the integrity and creative resources of R & F employees." All in all, it was a circumspect, not to say elevated, document; only a naïve outsider could wonder why several months had to be consumed in its preparation.

When not engrossed in these theoretical flights, Ruder & Finn formulate detailed guides on such subjects as "Launching A New Client," "Plan of Activity During First Month of Work for New Client" and "Press Conferences." These internal communiqués could well serve as texts for aspiring PR men, though they sound a trifle elementary for R & F's trained staff. Thus, on the question of when to hold a press conference: "The best excuse for a press conference is *valid news*. If you don't have valid news, you have to find a way to make it . . ."

Candor with the client is recommended, for many press conferences turn out to be disappointing affairs. "Tell him why you think the story may be weak, the advantages to be gained by simply getting the press in a good setting, and creating goodwill by the client among editors. He should know that even if no publicity will result—it will still be worthwhile." But there is an additional hazard; not only may little publicity result, but many of the invited guests may not appear. Thus it is better to warn the client "that at the last minute we may have to ask some members of his staff and our staff to attend the press conference in order to create the impression of a large group being present."

If the conference stands any chance of success, its setting and "mood" are very important. Ruder & Finn urge that "For business and trade it should be rather low key, dignified. . . . If it is a fashion or beauty show obviously it should be a feminine setting. For home furnishing—folksy. For gimmicks—off beat. Except for straight business where an aura of solidity is required, it is well worth putting time into the search for an off beat place. It does inject an element of surprise for jaded editors." There was equally sage advice on the cost of press conferences: "Whatever your budget—even though it seems like enough—it isn't. Always add $300 to $500 more and you may break even. If possible, bill the client directly. Saves R & F bookkeeping, time, headaches, and dunning."

In their pedagogic efforts, Ruder & Finn usually introduce a healthy dose of self-criticism. One of the more illuminating documents, written in 1956, in their collected staff reports involves the troublesome question of client turnover—a problem of concern to many of their competitors as well. In R & F's considered view, the first six months of an account are the most critical. When the relationship breaks down early in the game, it is likely to be due to "inadequate placement" or inadequate "liaison." Inadequate placement is a euphemism for not enough publicity, which is more likely to trouble a small company or one "relatively unsophisticated in public relations" than a larger or more knowing concern.

Unsuccessful liaison seems to be more baffling—for often R & F gives a lot of time to a client and assiduously cultivates the "key man" only to discover belatedly that "we weren't close enough to him or sensitive enough to see that we were not satisfying him."

If the account is lost after a year or eighteen months, R & F's diagnosis is that failure was likely to have come because "we have 'run out of gas' or have failed through *lack* of creative *planning*—either knowingly or unknowingly—to keep the client's interest alive in public relations." But there are other hazards as well: there are accounts "with which we never seemed 'to connect' . . . One possible explanation is that perhaps our selling job was either not thorough enough—or too thorough . . ." And there were others where the loss seemed motivated by circumstances beyond R & F's control—such as that of the client who "tried public relations experimentally and was unable really to afford the expense."

Satisfying a client, one can only conclude, is much more difficult than appeasing a capricious female. The only apparent solace is that for every client lost, there seem to be a half dozen good prospects waiting to be solicited.

In their relentless pursuit of self-knowledge, Ruder & Finn once went so far as to hire "a person from Radcliffe" to determine precisely what had been done for three clients over a period of a year. Finn candidly concedes, "It wasn't possible to discover what the value was—and even what actually happened." A similar frustration might of course also account for client turnover.

Despite the failure of the Radcliffe lady's project, the firm is still devoted to research and has financed a study at the New School for Social Research "to explore the nature of communications between people, the nature of public action and related subjects." They hope that the project will define "the problem" and eventually reach "a solution, or at least better understanding."

They find the question of ethics in public relations a fascinating subject; a number of top-level executive sessions have been devoted to its exploration. Dr. Louis Finkelstein, among other savants, has counseled the group in this undertaking.

Sample problem (from the minutes): ". . . many public relations men felt most uncomfortable about practices such as 'buying editors.'" Tentative solution, after discussion: "One standard for possible resolution of ethical conduct might be dependent on our own feeling if our action became public knowledge." Conclusion from a later meeting: "There are perhaps some absolutes. It was suggested that outright bribery should never be attempted. However, the definition of bribery is not always clear."

But, withal, Ruder & Finn have a disarming capacity for self-mockery. "We're either advance-type managers or we're nuts," Bill Ruder says genially. "We're not sure which."

Meantime, business is excellent.

9

*These
Call
Themselves
Press Agents*

Bernie Kamber, an accomplished movie press agent, had a little chore to do in Rome a few years ago. The star was Gina Lollobrigida, the film a three-million-dollar extravaganza known as *Trapeze* and the assignment to get a publicity break out of an outrageous demand, made by the Johnston office, that United Artists retouch Gina's stills. The bluenoses complained of too much cleavage.

The first inspiration that occurred to Kamber's colleagues was for Lollobrigida to sue the film's producers and distributors for "disfigurement of stills." In Rome Kamber decided that this was not a sufficiently good idea; Gina had been involved in so much litigation that something more was required. Then, in one of those blinding flashes which redeem the lives of press agents, Kamber thought of a gag for Gina to apply to the retouched stills: "It is my face—and the body of Gary Cooper."

But how to impress this gem on an inattentive public? A release would get little attention; clearly a stunt was called for. Kamber and Lollobrigida repaired to a local night club and in the presence of a rapt throng staged a loud and acrimonious argument. News of the spat soon got around town.

Next day Kamber hired a newspaperman, who could not use the story himself, to telephone the American correspondents in Rome and give them a friendly tip that Gina and Kamber had been quarreling about retouched stills—and that Gina would talk. Her phone soon began to buzz, and to all callers she stormed, "It is my face—and the body of Gary Cooper." She would show them the evidence to prove it.

Gina's cry and the horror perpetrated by the Johnston office—documented with before and after shots of the Lollobrigida façade—thereupon made headlines throughout the U.S. Kamber had earned his Roman holiday.

Such is the alchemy of the entertainment press agent, creating the glow of legend out of the accidents of history. Students of the communications arts sometimes wonder what the difference is between public relations and press agentry. "The size of the fees," says Arthur Cantor, a successful theatrical press agent.

This is, of course, only one of the differences. A PR man, if he is fortunate, helps a client shape corporate policy; a press agent harbors no such aspiration. Sufficient to him is the joy of seeing the clippings pile up. He does not mouth the solemnities so dearly loved by earnest PR counsel. Where the PR man creates "situations of reality" and "projects a corporate image," the press agent pulls stunts and plants column items. Nor does he mind being called a press agent. There is often a raffish and engaging air of huckstering about him. His candor can be appealing.

The entertainment world has spawned press agents since the

days of Barnum. Large colonies of them prosper in New York and Los Angeles, with smaller enclaves scattered elsewhere through the country. They are of several kinds:

Movie press agents, employed by the Hollywood companies;

TV and radio press agents, employed by the networks and local stations;

Theatrical press agents, who handle Broadway and off-Broadway productions;

Personal press agents, most of whose clients are individual performers—actors, dancers, singers, musicians and, on occasion, directors, producers and writers who want to be celebrated in the public prints. At times, a sound commercial instinct impels the desire for notoriety; just as frequently sheer ego aggrandizement motivates the craving.

The functions of the different types of press agent vary considerably. Unlike the personal press agent, the job of the movie specialist is not to pander to the vanity of the stars but to boom his company's pictures in all media—all over the world. His is a merchandising function, whose importance has been enhanced since television sliced away a good part of the traditional movie audience.

Technically, movie press agents undertake two main jobs—the regular purveying of news, features, photographs and ideas to the press; and "exploitation." Exploitation is the trade name for stunts designed to capture news space for a specific film. Despite its flamboyance, it is work which calls for a good deal of strategic consideration. A stunt can be clever and still not be worth the effort spent concocting it. The relevant rule is whether the product plugged is brought vividly enough to the attention of the desired audience.

Back in 1940, when Bernie Kamber was a fledgling in the business, he was in Boston exploiting five pictures released by United Artists. There was a convention of dentists in town, and it suddenly struck Kamber that he could ride their coattails into the nonentertainment pages of the newspapers. He had no trouble persuading the dentists' press agent—who was a dentist himself, and thus perhaps more susceptible—that movie stars had some of the finest-looking teeth in the world and should be a model to the nation's youth. Kamber made huge photographic blowups of the toothy smiles of the leading ladies in his five films, then posed a solemn dentist with a long blackboard pointer in front of the openmouthed display. Stories and pictures made the papers, as expected. On reflection, however, Kamber ruefully decided that he might have helped the dentists but he had not gotten much of a puff for his product. Dental hygiene was just too remote a gimmick.

At times, film promotion can avoid stunts and yet be effective. Such was the case, in 1955, with a low-budget picture called *Marty*, the story of the discontents and final triumph of a highly unromantic Bronx butcher. It was an off-beat item, appealing in its simple realism and the novelty of the unvarnished types it dealt with, but with apparently few possibilities for commercial success. The film was scheduled to open at a small theater in New York in April 1955; early in the year Kamber undertook to promote it. Exuberant press agentry was hardly called for; rather the technique was to convert the picture into a "sleeper" —to spread the word that a masterwork was quietly on its way. The method was a series of private screenings—approximately ninety in all in New York. (Another press agent handled a similar program on the West Coast.)

There is a certain cachet to the private screening; for some reason, even to the sophisticated, an invitation to a screening involves an amiable bit of flattery. Kamber's technique, he says, was merely to hold far more screenings than one normally would. He calculates that before the film opened, more than five thousand people had seen it privately in New York. "It was seen in high echelon circles and in low echelon circles; in the end we had five thousand press agents passing the word." He held a screening for Mrs. Toots Shor—who brought a flock of celebrities—and also one for all the waitresses in a Child's restaurant. When Kamber finished a cab ride, he was likely to invite the driver to a showing. The result was that by the time *Marty* opened, critics and columnists, as well as a broad swath of the public, had long been alerted. All could join in the pleasures of a personal discovery. The film eventually went on to gross millions. This technique, it need hardly be suggested, could not have worked if there was not a decent product to start with. But many fine art films, Kamber insists, fall by the wayside for lack of adequate nurture by press agents.

TV and radio press departments work much as movie press agents do. The networks have long regarded publicity as a major activity. At the National Broadcasting Company, when this reporter looked in on it recently, fifty-one people were employed in its New York press department, twenty-one in Hollywood—making this operation in entertainment press agentry as large as some of the PR departments of our major corporations. Like them, it is also headed by a vice-president, Sydney Eiges. The New York office covers the country west to Denver, with the Hollywood office taking over to the West Coast.

The basic product of the enterprise is a fat batch of releases and program listings, stapled together and dispatched by airmail to radio and TV editors or sent by special teletype circuit to the newspaper offices. A day's bundle is likely to contain news items, plot synopses, biographical sketches, cast listings— enough stuff to fill several columns of type. The material is collected by fifteen writers, who are regularly assigned to cover specific radio and TV shows. There is also a pool of photographers; a four-man group which funnels material to magazines; three people who plant items with columnists; three who publicize news and public affairs programs; and two who service the trade press. The photo department is indefatigable. Each week, never less than six photographs go out to each of 600 newspapers. In addition, there are special mailings to 110 papers which can use considerably more pictures. The column men also cover the whole country. They work the phone to reach the New York columnists, make special mailings of gossip items to the hinterland.

The operation is fairly straightforward. Television, as did radio in the past, generates enough consumer interest to provide a ready market for the sausage roll of information and puffery which NBC each day grinds out. Only a few newspapers around the country, for example, still demand that stations pay for program listings. In the early days of radio, this was a common practice.

At NBC, stunts and every kind of merchandising gimmick are in the hands of the exploitation department, headed by Al Rylander. Rylander does many things. He is responsible, for example, for plugging one NBC show on another NBC show— and, even better, on a CBS show. Sometimes these plugs are only parenthetic suggestions to the audience to catch a colleague's program, but often they are more elaborate—such as the "Win George Gobel for a Day Contest" he inspired on the "Today" show. The prize was Mr. Gobel, and the competition was among cities which for some reason wanted his presence. Cincinnati won.

Rylander also spends a good deal of time working up promotional tie-ins with manufacturers, department stores, civic groups and publications. It is a major coup when a national magazine can be persuaded to incorporate a TV plug in its own vast promotional outlay. The basic rule is reciprocity. Rylander recalls proudly that back in 1957, when the *Saturday Evening Post* ran an article about Dinah Shore, the singer was persuaded to hold up a copy of the magazine on her TV program and talk a bit about it. She had never allowed such a plug before, because of the objections of her sponsor. In return for Miss Shore's largesse (and assorted plugs on local NBC stations), the *Saturday Evening Post* reciprocated with truck banners, tack cards for newsstands and eighty-by-thirty-inch posters all touting Shore's NBC program as well as the magazine feature. Everybody gained by the deal—except possibly Dinah Shore's sponsor.

Apart from staff press agents and individual entrepreneurs who have their own clients, there are also along Broadway subcategories of press agents who work for other press agents: column men, who service the gossip columnists with reams of material, generally sending in three or four "free" items for each asterisked "client item"; stunt men, who hire out to perpetrate individual stunts; and pluggers.

Stunt men are, of course, highly imaginative fellows. The best known of the breed is probably Jim Moran, who among other accomplishments once sold an icebox to an Eskimo and found a needle in a haystack. Pluggers are less imaginative than persistent, specializing in a form of bribery hallowed by long tradition. Their assignment is to get free mention of their clients' wares on radio and TV shows; their modus operandi is to offer a writer or director a gift of cash, a case of whiskey or some other token of gratitude in exchange for a plug. Pluggers have an encyclopedic knowledge of which employees "take" and which do not; their trade flourishes despite stern prohibition by the networks.

Pluggers are either paid a flat fee per job or are reimbursed on a sliding scale—frequently ten dollars per point of the show's audience rating. This can be risky. One practitioner recently got his client an excellent plug on a TV show—only to discover that the program's rating had sunk so low on the night in question that his fee would not cover the cost of the case of Scotch he had pledged.

Over the last twenty-five years, entertainment press agentry has been considerably upgraded. Old-timers can remember when they went to work, fresh out of college, at $12 and $15 a week—and had to furnish their own typewriters. One hard taskmaster went so far as to install a pay telephone in his office, so that his hirelings would squander their own nickels. Client fees were low in the depression years, $25 to $30 a week being quite common. Today a successful press agent will get $100 to $300 a week per client—in rare instances as much as $500.

Theatrical press agents, who are strongly unionized, receive a minimum of $247.40 a week per show. If a man has two shows, the union requires him to hire an associate at $163.05 a week. Three shows (which is not uncommon) bring a total minimum of $742.20 a week, with the associate raised to $222.11. And capable practitioners usually get more than the minimum. "Legit" press agentry, however, is a modest operation, with a staff of six constituting a good-sized shop. Some theatrical press agents augment their income with outside clients.

Since the depression, the business has changed in other ways as well. Press agents are no less daring than in the past, but perhaps a little more chary of a downright lie. "In the old days," says veteran Sid Garfield, who is now CBS radio publicity director, "there was absolutely no ethics. The boys used to send out releases that George and Ira Gershwin were writing floor shows for the Village Grove Nut Club. Why, the Gershwins probably never heard of the Village Grove Nut Club. Today I'd like to see anyone take in vain the name of a Porter or Hammerstein or Irving Berlin."

Dissembling can have its rewards, however. On one occasion, a press agent had to publicize a restaurant which sadly lacked a floor show. To break into the night club columns, he blithely invented a dance team and sent around rapturous accounts of its performance. Dance team and restaurant were promptly noted, but one columnist later took umbrage at something the press agent had done. To square accounts, he printed a scathing review of the mythical dance team. The press agent was delighted: two client mentions for the sweat of one.

The years of prosperity have also seen an exuberant development of a costly device more sparingly employed in the thirties—the press junket. Piling a group of reporters and columnists into a plane, whisking them in an alcoholic cloud several thousand miles to the scene of some "staged event," wining and dining them in agreeable surroundings will always produce a predictable volume of flattering press notices. A few ingrates may not respond with plugs, but these miserable creatures are unlikely to be invited again.

The volume of press copy that a junket can generate—especially if there is something to write about—is often well worth the expense. In November 1957, for example, NBC flew seventy-three television editors to Hollywood for a week-long junket (another thirty-two joined the party there). Total cost was a little more than $25,000, including the chartering of a plane, hotel rooms, meals and travel insurance for each guest. It was an energetic frolic. NBC's guests toured its studios, interrogated top executives at a press conference, watched the filming of television serials, were entertained at the homes of Alfred Hitchcock, Dinah Shore and Bob Hope, met several other stars and on occasion were photographed with them to impress hometown readers. When the party was over, NBC counted 20,000 words a day telegraphed by its guests out of the junket's press room; doubtless thousands more went by mail. For a week, it had gotten a big play on virtually every important television page in the country—though a minority of papers, which do not approve of junkets, would not send reporters.

To its devotees, press agentry has many advantages. Richard Maney, the most celebrated of theatrical press agents, was recently asked about the satisfactions of his calling. Maney grinned broadly. "To be honest," he said, "I've never found a way to make a living in an easier fashion.

"Our bosses probably don't know what the hell we're up to. You seldom see your employer or hear from him. Why, I've only seen Herman Levin [the producer of *My Fair Lady*] three times in the last year. In short, press agents have greater liberty and take less benzedrine than anybody in the theater."

The hours are wonderful, Maney added. He works only from 10:30 A.M. to 5 P.M., after which—unless he has to visit a client's play—he can then embark for his home in the country. And over the previous twenty-five years, he calculated that he had averaged thirty thousand dollars a year—with very little overhead. He has a one-room office, a mimeograph machine and no secretary.

By no means do all Broadway press agents do this well. Some have to grub frantically for a living. And even the successful ones have usually gone through a bleak apprenticeship. The professional chronicle of Lee Solters is typical. Solters is now thirty-nine, a chubby, quick-moving man, with none of the brass generally associated with his trade. He is now senior partner in a flourishing operation known as Solters, O'Rourke and Sabinson, which has a staff of eleven and occupies a good-sized office on West 44th Street.

Like many of the new model press agents, Solters studied journalism in college. His ambition was to be a sports writer (to see the games free). At New York University, he was invariably publicity chairman of the proms (to get a free ticket). This experience gave him a meager immersion in press agentry. When he was graduated in 1941, he decided to look for a job in the field. He prudently did not try for a newspaper job: "I didn't know a soul on the papers."

For six months, he called on publicity firms, methodically going down the alphabetical listings in the classified directory. No one bid for his services. "Then I changed my tactics. I started with the bottom of the list—Zimmerman & Garfield." Providentially, Zimmerman & Garfield hired him. "I got a job on a Thursday," Solters recalls. "On Monday they decided to dissolve the partnership."

Z & G were agreeable enough to recommend him to another firm, operated by Leo Guild and Ezra Goodman. They grabbed him. The next day Solters got a telegram announcing that Guild and Goodman had broken up.

Sid Garfield then sent the ever-hopeful Solters to Sobel and Hartman, who finally provided steady employment—at fifteen dollars a week. Solters remained ten months, then got a job with Ed Wiener, served in the army, held two other jobs with Broadway press agents. By 1948, he was ready to strike out for himself.

His first important client—the keystone of every promising publicity operation—was comedian Jack Gilford. Solters did an energetic job for Gilford, who showed his appreciation by introducing him to Robert Q. Lewis' producer. Lewis, whose renown was considerably greater than Gilford's, became a Very Important Client. Some of his prestige inevitably rubbed off on his press agent. Other clients flocked in. In 1951, Solters acquired Jimmy O'Rourke as a partner, and in 1956, Harvey Sabinson.

The Solters combine now has about fifteen clients at fees ranging from $150 to $300 a week—among them the McGuire Sisters, Walter Slezak, Hume Cronyn, Erroll Garner, Jessica Tandy, Sal Mineo, Constance Bennett, Lisa Kirk, and of course Robert Q. Lewis. Solters' proudest boast, in a flighty industry, is that Lewis has been with him for eleven years. Marge and Gower Champion stayed for eight. That is success. He also earns $25,000 a year.

Although a press agent who has arrived can make considerably more money than his opposite numbers on the newspapers, there are certain drawbacks to the trade. Unsophisticated or temperamental clients can make impossible demands. The dissatisfied client is the subject of a number of wry jokes.

"Whatever happened to my sense of humor?" an aggrieved client complained to his press agent when he dropped out of the columns for several days.

"Don't worry," the press agent said soothingly, "everybody's talking about you."

"What are they saying?" demanded the client.

"They're all asking what happened to you."

According to Richard Maney, "The real problems are the newcomers among producers. They are always wondering why their latest pronouncement isn't on page one of the *Times*. Some of these characters have the quaintest notion of what constitutes news."

Some years ago, a musician, then conducting an orchestra at the Roxy Theater in New York, asked his press agent to arrange a press conference. The p.a. knew that he could get the client's communiqué into the papers, but that city desks were hardly likely to regard it as sufficiently momentous to require attendance at a press conference. The solution was to fake a press conference, with several other press agents posing as reporters. The story appeared in the papers, as anticipated, and the client was never the wiser.

Many clients also demand a variety of personal attentions from their press agents; the duties are subsumed under the heading of "servicing a client." They can be a sorry affliction. "I have known press agents," says a veteran practitioner, "who have to scurry around to get mink coats for their clients at wholesale prices, who take the client's dog to the veterinarian, and who visit the client's mother in the nursing home when the client can't spare the time. It can be a hell of a life."

Sensitive souls also find it demeaning, on occasion, continually to have to ask favors of the press. Insensitive souls indulge in a practice known, not very figuratively, as "crying." The press agent calls up a friendly reporter or editor and informs him, with many a throb in the voice, that he will lose his client—or his job—if he does not get a decent hunk of space. Within five minutes, the newspaperman feels like a heel; it may take a great exertion of moral authority to resist the assault.

To the successful, however, the pleasures of press agentry far outweigh its dissatisfactions. Not only can the pay be good, but the pursuit has all the attractions of a game, an amiable battle of wits between the press agent and the press.

Some years ago, in an incredible reversal of tradition, a Broadway columnist on the New York *Daily News* announced that he would no longer print gags attributed to clients by press agents. Press agent Bernie Green regarded this as a challenge which could not be resisted. He had reason to believe that the columnist did not know of his client, band leader Al Donahue, and so Green merely rang up and announced: "My name is Al Donahue. I'm a press agent and I have a client named Bernie Green." He read off his gag, only to be informed that the columnist would credit it to press agent Donahue but not to client Green. It so appeared—a sweet moment of triumph.

Such a ruse cannot be tried too often; the favor of columnists is too important to any press agent handling personalities. The art of cultivating columnists largely involves becoming friendly enough to win frequent plugs—but not becoming so identified with any particular columnist as to court rejection by his rivals. To gain acceptance by a columnist, a press agent will study his crotchets as well as his verbal mannerisms, sometimes feeding him derogatory items about people he dislikes and always sending him material modeled so closely after his style that, if need be, it can be printed verbatim.

There is a bond of mutual dependence, of course, between gossip columnist and press agent: without the latter, the wells of gossip would almost dry up. A knowledgeable press agent can often read a column and tell you the likely source of almost every item in it. He may slip up, of course, when a columnist switches attribution of a gag from a client to a more newsworthy name. In the trade, this is regarded as dirty pool.

One of the pleasures of working the columns is that an item need have only a remote resemblance to the truth; no one strenuously objects. But sometimes a press agent can overreach himself. Some years ago, an eager beaver planted an item that his client, a celebrated radio writer, was unable to get his mother to the country for the summer; she preferred to vacation in her old Jewish haunts on the lower East Side. The item was just a bit too good—for one of the wire services subsequently phoned the press agent with the suggestion of a picture layout. A safari to the Catskills had to be hastily organized to dislodge the writer's protesting mother and convey her to the East Side before the photographer arrived.

The manipulative joys of the successful stunt are perhaps the high point of the press agent's life. In March 1958, a young lady in the audience of John Osborne's *Look Back in Anger* clambered onto the stage and took a few pokes at the male lead. "The way you've been treating that woman!" she screamed at the actor. "My husband did the same thing to me. He left me! He left me!" She was hauled off into the wings and the curtain rung down. The local newspapers gave a big play to the incident, with no suggestion that there was anything synthetic in it.

Not until two days later did the intelligence reach print that stunt man Jim Moran had masterminded the assault. By that time, *Look Back in Anger*, which had been sagging at the box office, had reaped the benefit of several columns of free advertising and Moran could accept the accolades of his admirers.

If the idea of a stunt is clever enough, an indulgent press will often forgive the most apparent contrivance. Some years ago, a passenger entered a New York taxi and told the driver, "Take me to Juarez." He thereupon fell asleep and awoke to find himself in Philadelphia. To his horror, he discovered that the driver was on his way to Juarez, Mexico, whereas the passenger had merely wanted to go to the Warner Brothers film of that name playing in New York. The ensuing dispute brought the pair into court, and the proceedings were duly headlined in the press. It was all a transparent stunt on behalf of the movie, but no one seemed to mind.

At times, a press agent will reach very far afield. One practitioner, casting about for ways of publicizing a professional strong man, happened to run into a friend seeking a divorce. The court papers had not yet been filed, and the press agent, thinking fast, offered to underwrite the cost of the divorce if the husband would charge that the p.a.'s client had alienated his wife's affections. The gimmick was that she kept large photographs of the strong man around her bedroom and the husband found it all terribly humiliating. The tabloids regarded this as one of the juiciest tales in weeks.

The contrived arrest is a far more frequent prop. Years ago, when he was publicizing Mike Todd's *The Hot Mikado*, press agent Bill Doll managed to get dancer Bill Robinson arrested on a Broadway street corner. Robinson had collected an admiring crowd, and thereby blocked traffic, while watching himself do a jig on an animated advertising screen overhead. The gag was sure fire: "arrested for watching himself dance."

Unhappily, one cannot always mobilize the long arm of the law. Back in 1957, NBC put on a show called "Festival of Magic," in which famous magicians from all over the world participated. Al Rylander dreamed up a death-defying little adventure to get a publicity break. One of his charges was a magician from India who rode a bicycle blindfolded. Rylander brought machine, blindfold and bicycle over to Seventh Avenue, a one-way street, and had the daring fellow pedal against the traffic. The only difficulty was that Rylander could not find a cop to give his magician a ticket. Police Commissioner Kennedy, he was politely informed, would be aggrieved at any officer who knowingly lent himself to a publicity stunt. Such sophistication could easily drive press agents out of business.

Subterfuge is not always necessary to carry off a successful stunt. Some years ago, when he was in the movie field, Rylander had an assignment to publicize the film *The Caine Mutiny*. At the time, the biggest entertainment attraction in the country was the television rendition of the Army-McCarthy hearings. Rylander decided to insinuate a plug for his film.

The first step was to have a Washington press agent cultivate one of Senator Karl Mundt's secretaries. When the pleasantries were done, the p.a. wangled an introduction to Mundt, the chairman of the committee, and asked him to act as host at a private screening of *The Caine Mutiny* for the committee members and staff. Mundt agreed. The press agent then secured a model of the *Caine* and presented it to the senator before the committee's session got under way one day. When the hearing went on the air, Senator Mundt genially pointed to the ship model on the table in front of him and invited the committee members to the screening. Millions of people, presumably, heard the plug.

None of the senators objected to the commercial intrusion. Indeed, Senator McCarthy quipped: "Do you mean the Caine Mutiny or the Cohn Mutiny?"

What press agent could ask for more?

10

Corporation PR: No Midget on the Knee

"This is not a midget that you put on J. P. Morgan's knee every other day to solve a problem. We just do from day to day what comes naturally, with as little trickery and manipulation as possible." Thus Charles F. Moore, Jr., of the Ford Motor Company, characterizing the operation of his far-flung public relations department.

Moore could have been speaking as well for the thousands of PR operations in American corporations here and abroad. Public relations in the corporation, as PR men are fond of repeating, is a "function of management." It is the function of manufacturing good will with the same relentless attention to detail as is devoted to the manufacture of motorcars, kitchen sinks, oil pumps and plastic zippers. It is not only an arm of management but an adjunct to salesmanship, a backstop to labor relations, a tool of stockholder relations and a handmaiden to community relations. It is by and large a straightforward, sober operation.

It is often sober to the point of dullness, solemn to the point of stuffiness. It is usually characterized by less "trickery and manipulation" than some of the operations of the independent PR firms, but as Moore suggests, there is often a "little" of these imaginative qualities. A small boon, one would imagine, which relieves the tedium both for the practitioner and the dispassionate observer.

The corporate PR department, as a mass phenomenon, is of relatively recent vintage. A few corporations began such operations before the First World War, but throughout the twenties and much of the thirties the outside consulting firm dominated the field of business public relations. On occasion, a company would first hire a consultant, then with his assistance set up its own department. U. S. Steel has only had a PR department since 1936, Standard Oil (New Jersey) since 1942, American Cyanamid since 1956.

The wholesale disesteem which befell American business, in the depths of the depression, provided the motive force for the establishment of PR departments in a number of large corporations. Charles Huse, second in command of the public relations department at U. S. Steel, vividly recalls the atmosphere when our largest steel producer began concerted efforts to win public favor. "If you look back at 1936, at that time the so-called political revolution was in effect. Much of the suspicion about big business arose from the fact that nobody knew what went on inside. There were high fences around the plants—no one went in except the workmen. Newer management realized that it had to operate in a goldfish bowl." One of U. S. Steel's first moves, after this revelation broke over it, was to provide conducted tours of the plant goldfish bowls for any citizens who might be curious.

The Borden Company was facing similar problems in the mid-thirties. Milton Fairman, Borden's PR chief, can now view the situation with Olympian detachment, but at the time it was painful. "The farmers were distressed. You had noisy consumer groups in New York, Chicago, Detroit, agitating about the 'milk trust.' Around the country newspaper editorials were screaming about the price of milk being too high." Plainly a PR department was needed "to give the public the facts" about the complex economics of milk.

The depression jitters was of course not the only inspiration for the emergence of public relations as a specialized function within the corporate hierarchy. Through past blunders, a company might find itself in bad odor with the public, even in an era when business as a whole was regarded tolerantly. Such was the case, as previously mentioned, with the Ford Motor Company, which by 1945, when young Henry Ford came in as president, had achieved an awesome reputation for corporate delinquency under the eccentric tutelage of his grandfather. An expanded public relations program was among the many innovations which young Henry undertook soon after he assumed control.

There were other corporations, as well, which merely succumbed to the incessant propaganda of the PR specialist. As one executive has put it, "Some firms buy public relations just because they have a vague idea it's a good thing to have. Everybody else has it—and then someone on the board will say, 'Don't you know PR is a tool of modern management?' Who wants to be backward? It's something like putting in IBM machines when four bookkeepers with pencils can do the job."

The corporate PR department undertakes some of the same activities for which an outside consulting firm may be qualified, but there are marked dissimilarities between the two operations. For one thing, a different atmosphere is apparent in the organization. The corporate department head has the inestimable advantage of not being dependent on a flow of new clients. He faces the normal necessity of satisfying his boss and keeping his job, but there is not the same anxiety felt by the consultant lest the client be displeased. If something goes wrong, corporations are a bit quicker to switch consulting firms than to lop off heads in their own departments. (In a recession, budgets may be cut in either case, though in the 1957–58 recession public relations showed a remarkable stability, according to the *Public Relations News*.) All of which means that the PR department of the large corporation operates in a considerably more relaxed setting than the outside consultant.

Not only is there none of the exertion attendant on attracting new clients, but the press is usually courted with considerably less razzle-dazzle. At least in the case of the larger corporations, a news break is not especially difficult to arrange. Big business is news; any major gambit on the part of General Motors, U. S. Steel, Standard Oil or American Airlines will elicit a predictable response from the media. Smaller companies, of course, have to work a bit harder to get into the headlines. The tendency among corporate personnel, however, is for a more discreet handling of the press. If more exuberant overtures are required, the corporation is likely to delegate the responsibility to an outside PR firm.

Certain advantages and disabilities seem to be evenly balanced between the inside department and the outside consultant. The staff PR man, at least on the higher levels, often has a more intimate knowledge of the mechanics of his company and the interplay of its politics and thus may be more effective in helping shape policies. He may also suffer less resentment for being a visionary interloper among hardheaded businessmen; if at all deft, he can win acceptance as a member of the "team." The outside consultant has a harder time attaining this status. On the other hand, he is presumed to have the compensating advantages of greater objectivity and independence. Viewing the corporate profile from the outside, he can more readily glimpse its blemishes. Such, at least, is the theory. But the vigor with which he delivers his critique may well be affected by apprehension lest he prejudice his tenure. Considerable discretion may be called for.

The discretion of the corporate PR operation takes many other forms as well. A certain solemnity and deliberateness characterizes the corporate gesture. It is the rare and antediluvian industrial figure—a Robert Young or a Cyrus Eaton in the old days —who flails about in an uninhibited fashion in the public prints. Milton Fairman, for one, is still struck by the restraint of the executive manner in business; in the thirties, before he went to work for the Borden Company, he was a press agent for Harold Ickes, a master of inventive vituperation. "When I was with Ickes," Fairman recalls, "we always took the headlines. Huey Long attacked the Roosevelt administration; the next day Ickes said that Long suffered from intellectual B.O. When Bob Moses hit at Ickes on the issue of the Triboro Bridge, Ickes was even more abusive—and of course we made the headlines. But you can't do that in a business. If a businessman wanted to let loose such an attack, one would wonder what would the stockholders think, what would the bankers think, what would our principal customers think—would it be taken as evidence of emotional instability? Besides, most businessmen aren't temperamentally prepared for such tactics."

The public relations goals of corporations fall into a common pattern. The over-all objective, as suggested in the first chapter, is institutional acceptance—a diligent marketing of a flattering image among a company's customers, stockholders, employees and the public at large. A closely allied objective, for companies which manufacture consumer products, is moving merchandise. This means product publicity—the one area where a stunt may be decently perpetrated.

The problem of institutional acceptance is of course of greatest concern to large corporations. (The small company is likely only to be seeking recognition.) At mid-century, the public certainly views big business more indulgently than in the thirties, but many difficulties remain. Anthony DeLorenzo, vice-president in charge of public relations at General Motors, states that his major public relations problem is "bigness." The solution? "We don't try to make ourselves look small, but to look good." Meantime, the government compounds the problem by starting a grand jury investigation of possible antitrust violations.

The problem of justifying size in a country whose folk myths celebrate the private entrepreneur is one shared by all our corporate hierarchs. Bigness becomes even more embarrassing when charges echo through the land that prices and profits are too high. Recent attacks by Democratic politicians on the rigidities of "administered prices," a concept originated by Gardner Means, forced corporate PR departments to devote thousands of man-hours to rebuttal and self-defense.

The defensive campaign takes many forms. U. S. Steel maintains a mailing list of 100,000 "opinion leaders" around the country to whom it regularly sends mailings of speeches by company executives. The mass public is approached by way of the U. S. Steel Hour, a popular TV program produced by the

Theater Guild. Each show contains one "institutional" commercial, which is frequently devoted to "economic education."

Inculcating the economic facts of life in two and a half minutes is no easy matter, but U. S. Steel gives it a good try. The general approach can be suggested by one capsule lecture in 1958, dramatized by puppets, about what happens to its revenues. At the outset, the audience is told that "For the carbon and alloy steel you bought this year, you paid 7¾ cents a pound on the average"—a statement which illustrates the first principle of how to talk about prices and profits: keep the magnitudes small. Steel is of course bought by the ton rather than by the pound, but per ton prices would look too big.

After this introduction, the audience is shown a stack of coins representing each dollar of U. S. Steel's income and is informed how it was disposed of the previous year: 42½ cents "went to and for our employees"; suppliers got 30 cents; "Father Time" (depreciation allowable by the tax authorities) took 6 cents; taxes claimed 12 cents—leaving a mere 9½ cents. (Another bit of sleight of hand: taxes are regarded as costs, though the bulk of them are taxes on profits. But again the sum is smaller if one deals with net rather than gross profit.)

Finally, of the 9½ cents left, 2 cents more had to be allocated to depreciation—leaving "only 7½ cents of real profit. Of this 7½ cents, 4 cents went to over 300,000 share-owners in the form of dividends. This is the 4 cents they earned for the use of all the plants, tools, furnaces, mills and machines they provided." Obviously, only a pittance. The remaining 3½ cents went "to pay for new research facilities, to discover and develop new and better raw materials, and to finance the improvements necessary to provide for the growing needs of a growing nation."

By this time, U. S. Steel almost looks like a charitable enterprise. If the steelworkers' union wrote the commercial, one would surmise that the same figures would be rearranged to emphasize that in 1957 the company's profits before taxes were 21½ per cent of dollar volume. Just another way of saying the same thing.

Apart from justifying profits, there are a host of other PR problems which bedevil the corporation. Few more ticklish situations are encountered than when a company must close a plant at which thousands are employed. Charges of air and stream pollution are another headache. If a labor dispute is brewing, effective "communication" with the employees is usually a PR responsibility. An accident at a plant always poses a challenge: how to satisfy the papers and yet minimize the unfavorable publicity.

The corporate PR approach is usually a long-range one. The theory is that if the company, over a period of time, is swathed in layers of good will, it will not be damaged by an occasional fusillade of abuse. Thus the enormous attention paid to charitable projects in plant communities, the provision of scholarships to deserving students, the production of educational aids for use in the schools, the assiduous cultivation of good relations with stockholders. The stockholders, when effectively indoctrinated, are in themselves a valuable PR tool for use against an unsympathetic government. As John W. Hill observed in his book, *Corporate Public Relations,* as a result of "sound" PR programs, "Stockholders have increasingly become vocal against unwise regulatory measures and against excessively high taxes on personal incomes, dividends, and corporation's enterprise. It is possible now to expect truly substantial waves of protest against anti-business measures and stifling taxes."

The full range of industry's PR efforts are on display at the Ford Motor Company. The status of a PR operation is often measured by the rank of its chief: Charles Moore, who oversees both advertising and public relations, has the title of vice-president and sits on the company's administrative committee. Thus, at Ford, PR has a "voice" at the highest level of management. In the person of Moore, a hearty, informal type with a gift for imaginative epithet, the voice is exceptionally vigorous. Moore also has a good deal of money at his disposal, but Ford, like most corporations, will not reveal its PR budget.

Heading the public relations staff under Moore is Theodore H. Mecke, Jr., an ex-newspaperman in his mid-thirties who is General Public Relations Manager. He supervises the work of some two hundred people ("professionals" and clericals) who staff the headquarters office in Dearborn and nine branch offices —in Atlanta, Chicago, Cleveland, Dallas, Kansas City, Los Angeles, New York, San Francisco and Washington. Until a reorganization in April 1959, he also had responsibility for the Civic and Governmental Affairs Office, which now reports directly to Moore.

The entire operation can serve as a textbook illustration of how far public relations has spread from its origins in simple press agentry. Ford's PR program takes account of every conceivable juncture where the company impinges on the public consciousness—beginning with stockholder relations.

The Civic Affairs Office, for example, includes an Associate for Dealer Information, an Associate for Civic Groups and Lansing Representative ("a lobbyist at the state capitol," says Mecke), a Washington office ("the manager is also a lobbyist"), an Associate for State Government and another for Municipal Government ("not lobbyists but fellows who follow developments").

Also part of the civic affairs setup is a Community Relations Department and a Traffic Safety and Highway Improvement

Department. All specialize in those disinterested expressions of benevolence designed to prove to the cynical that the Ford Motor Company is as public-spirited as it is profitable.

The mass production of benevolence takes many forms. The Community Relations Department guides the efforts of community relations committees which operate out of each of Ford's regional PR offices. These local committees, made up of plant executives in the area, arrange for Ford's participation in local affairs, handle contributions to Community Chests, donate automotive equipment to trade schools and generally supervise the mundane chores of a good-neighbor policy.

Traffic Safety and Highway Improvement, among other things, produces and distributes "Driver Education" films. Their big market is in the schools. "Automatic Transmissions," "Care of the Car," "Driving At Night" are among the titles which are annually viewed by several million people. "What we get out of this is highly theoretical," Ted Mecke concedes. "Our products are seen, but often by kids who won't be in the market for them for five years. On the other hand, we create the impression that we're mindful of our responsibility to promote safe driving. We just don't know whether it pays off."

Mecke also has an Educational Affairs Department, which deals with secondary schools and institutions of higher learning on all matters not involving automobile safety. A raft of literature, prepared by a sister department—Research and Information—is funneled out to the schools. Some items indulge in candid self-glorification, among them a forty-page booklet entitled "Ford Today" and a larger treatment of "The Evolution of Mass Production" ("How mass production was originated and developed and the significance of Ford's part in making it a vital part of our daily lives").

Other materials grind no corporate axes. There are a series of charts on the auto industry ("How An Automobile Is Designed," "How An Automobile Is Engineered"), a booklet on how "A Car Is Born," a wall poster on "Dream Cars." A number of pamphlets on career guidance are also offered, as well as a very popular item called "How Long Is A Rod," which explains the origins of the standards of linear measure.

Educational Affairs also runs forums, distributes films, reprints of speeches by Ford executives and handles the Industrial Arts Awards program. This is a nationwide competition, with prizes totaling fifty thousand dollars a year, for imaginative gadgetry fabricated in the industrial craft shops of the nation's high schools. "This again is a program which doesn't have high visibility," says Mecke, "but it encourages craftsmanship and produces a good impression of Ford at least among industrial arts teachers and students. And we depend on these kids to man our factories."

On Mecke's organization chart, a prominent place is occupied by the Public Communications Office, which has four subordinate units. There is a Photographic Department, whose services are available to the entire company, a News Department, a Research and Information Department and a Radio-TV News and Motion Picture Department.

The latter unit handles contacts with networks and local stations and also produces films, for use on TV and at community meetings. Many of these productions seem quite remote from the automobile industry. Most popular is a thirty-three minute color item called "The American Cowboy"; there is also a celebration of the "American Farmer," a film on the "State Trooper," another urging citizens to vote, several travelogues and an examination of "Watercolor and Printers Ink." Mention of the Ford

Motor Company is made at the beginning and end of each film. "That's what we presumably get out of it," says Mecke. "Twenty-six million people saw these films in 1957, exclusive of television, but we don't know how much impact they had. There are a lot of things we don't know about this business."

The Research and Information Department acts as custodian of the Ford Archives, prepares printed materials and serves as Ford's letter-answering service to the general public. As is the case with any corporation which has become a legend in the land, Ford receives a staggering volume of nonbusiness mail from admirers young and old. In the first eleven months of 1958, more than 130,000 letters and post cards flooded in.

Thousands of letters requested specific pieces of literature. Others—the number is some 3,600 a year—asked "old car" questions. Typical is the letter with photograph attached, inquiring about the vintage of the car. More ardent fans would request information on how to restore old-model cars (Ford has licensed a San Francisco firm to supply reproductions of ancient manuals).

A great number of correspondents have an exaggerated notion of Ford's largesse. A standard gambit is "I understand that if I drive a 1922 Model T to Dearborn, you'll give me a Thunderbird." At intervals, for reasons which are totally unclear, there comes a flurry of queries as to whether the Ford Motor Company will provide a new car in return for a 1943 copper penny—or for four dimes with mint marks spelling out FORD. And then there is the more modest request, "Dear Mr. Ford, please send me a gold piece." However bizarre, each letter receives a reply, if only a printed post card. "These people are gold," says one PR executive. "There is no better captive audience."

The News Department addresses a decidedly noncaptive

audience—newspapers, magazines and wire services. The department numbers fourteen people, eight of them "professionals," and is organized on the pattern of a newspaper city room, with reporters detailed to specific "beats" or general assignment. Its time is equally divided between answering queries from the media and originating its own copy; around forty-five releases are issued each month. "When we cover, we cover, just as a city desk would," boasts Jack Clarke, chief of public information. "In our end of the business, we have people experienced in news rather than in public relations. We find we come off better if we tell the bad as well as the good. It's always true that if you have a bad story, you're better off to take your beating and get out fast."

While Clarke's staff hardly indulges in gratuitous exposés—of a sort a city desk might suggest—it is true that it makes no unseemly efforts to hide unpalatable facts. At times, Ford's cordiality to an inquiring press can boomerang. Back in 1949–50, there was a flurry of arrests of company employees involved in in-plant gambling rings. Such operations were not confined to Ford, but Ford was the only major auto company in the Detroit area to concede that the problem was significant and to allow reporters to interview whomever they wished on the subject. The other companies, as this writer can testify, denied that they were at all troubled by gambling and refused any help in digging out the story. The consequence was that newspaper and magazine accounts concentrated on delinquency at Ford; the rest of the industry looked relatively good.

This was not the only occasion when one of Ford's public relations gambits had unexpected consequences. There is little doubt that the company won enormous public favor through the benefactions of the Ford Foundation. But one of its offshoots—

the Fund for the Republic—caused painful embarrassment. The fund was dedicated to educational efforts to preserve and extend civil liberties in America. Once it was established, with a grant of fifteen million dollars, it was totally independent of the Ford Foundation—and, of course, of the Ford Motor Company. But this independence brought little solace when the fund and its chief executive, Robert Hutchins, became engaged in public controversy—over such matters as the award it once gave to a library board which refused to fire an employee who had taken the Fifth Amendment. Some of Hutchins' pronouncements distressed civil libertarians as well as the far right fringe. Most of the criticism, however, came from the latter quarter, which showed a dismaying inability to distinguish between Mr. Hutchins in New York and the auto company in Dearborn.

Boycott threats were heard in southern states, and there were also reports that some service stations were refusing to sell gasoline to owners of Ford cars. Public relations efforts, so far as one could tell, availed little to redress the situation. Protesting customers were informed that the Ford Motor Company had no hand in the Fund for the Republic and, when opportunity afforded, speakers were sent to the South to talk about the affirmative aspects of Ford's operation. "It's a problem that still hasn't been solved," says Charles Moore. "You can't solve it with a speech by Henry or a press release." The real therapy will have to be the passage of time.

Normally, the PR department feels on safer ground in maneuvering for public support. In 1958, the automobile industry was in acute distress: not only had sales and earnings declined steeply in a recession year, but there was mounting criticism that Detroit was out of tune with the American public, producing a car that was too large, too powerful, and too glittering for the average consumer. Even the President of the United States, at a press conference, took an unkind poke at the auto manufacturers.

"What all the criticism came down to," says Moore, "was that a bunch of arrogant bastards sit out here in Detroit and if they should decide to put pyramids on top of cars, the public would goddam well have to take it. The Ford Motor Company was especially sensitive because we spend a small fortune on consumer research—much more than on public relations."

To efface any impression of arrogance, a major PR gesture was obviously called for. This took the form of a widely publicized Consumers' Conference, convened by Ford in October 1958. As the staff's "Program Treatment and Outline" put it, the conference was "aimed at creating a national impression that the 1959 Ford car is the product of a tremendous, long-range, continuing and grass-roots effort to find out exactly what the consumer says he wants." Four hundred "representative" consumers, from all parts of the country, were brought to Detroit to help create that impression. Their comments, of course, could no longer affect the 1959 car, which was about to go on the market, but the resultant hoopla was nonetheless valuable. Moreover, consumer guidance could always be used for the 1960 cars.

Working to an elaborate schedule, Ford's PR staff exploited every publicity angle in their cross-country operation. First, in August, came a national announcement of the conference; the release noted that George Gallup was picking the four hundred cities to be represented. (Gallup had been hired, Moore explains, in order to make the selection "nonsuspect.") Next, in September, there followed local and regional stories when announcement was made of the selection of the four hundred towns. Some days later, another flurry of local stories appeared when each of the four hundred panelists was named.

Then came the conference on October 8 and 9, during which the panelists toured the Ford plant, heard lectures on consumer research and styling, queried Ford executives, watched a Test Track Demonstration, filled out questionnaires and attended a round of cocktail parties, lunches and dinners. More home-town stories were dispatched by Ford's indefatigable press agents, together with a photograph of each panelist in earnest conversation with a Ford vice-president. In some cases, TV "clips" were also shot for use on home-town stations.

After the conference ended, the returning panelists naturally informed the local press of their impressions of the motor capital. Nor was this all. Another newsbreak occurred when a local Ford dealer loaned each panelist a new '59 Ford, for a month's trial run. This was billed as "a unique consumer road test, one of the most extensive in history." After the month was over, the panelists were allowed to purchase the cars at used-model prices; 303 of the 400 availed themselves of the privilege. Meantime, they all apprised Ford of their impressions of the new car in lengthy questionnaires. By January, Ford was able to announce triumphantly that 84 per cent of the panelists regarded the Ford as the best-looking car in the field and 72 per cent thought it the most comfortable. The release added that "the characteristics the panelists liked best about the 1959 Fords correlated closely with the style and operating improvements which, on October 8, they said they wanted for the future." That was triumph enough.

Ambitious though it was, the Consumers' Conference was by no means the biggest "created event" undertaken by Moore's department. That distinction goes to Ford's fiftieth anniversary celebration in 1953, a classic of its kind. Two years of preparation preceded nine months of the most varied activities. High point of the festivities was **a t**wo-hour television show, broadcast over both the NBC and CBS networks and viewed in an estimated sixteen million homes. So dense a saturation could hardly be achieved in the other media, but Ford came close. In the space of six months, *Life* carried four stories on the Ford anniversary, one of them fourteen pages long. Two articles each appeared in *Look*, *Time* and *Newsweek*, one each in the *Saturday Evening Post*, *Cosmopolitan*, *Fortune* and the *Reader's Digest*. Six institutional ads were also published in magazines with a total circulation of eighty-two million.

In a three-month period, newspaper clippings were estimated at 59,000 column inches—which is equal to 332 pages of the New York *Times*. Some 483,000 copies of a hard-cover book, *Ford at Fifty*, were distributed, as well as nearly 2,400,000 calendars, with Norman Rockwell illustrations. A film, "The American Road," was viewed by 550,000 people in a four-month period. There were 34 Dealer Anniversary Dinners around the country, with a total attendance of 21,685; some 3,900 dealers held open houses. There was also a 1,000-mile Model-T race in Argentina, and in India Ford customers were presented with souvenir key rings bearing the anniversary medallion.

It was a huge success, according to Ford's PR experts, but how to measure the extent of it? One way was by the dollar value of the free publicity received—estimated to be worth $2,200,000 if bought at space rates. Another was by the response of dealers in the field, who reported that their morale had been substantially boosted "for the strenuous days ahead." But what was especially pleasing, according to the official chronicle of the proceedings, was the fact that "Out of all the material pub-

lished during the anniversary year there has begun to emerge a
new image of Henry Ford and his impact on our way of life.
In reviewing the hundreds of pictures and thousands of words,
it is significant that an almost infinitesimal amount is derogatory
in character. And yet Henry Ford has been considered a controversial figure by many for years." Thus does public relations
its marvels perform.

When one moves away from the corporate center to Ford's
outlying PR offices, a somewhat more exuberant atmosphere is
encountered. The regional offices are supposed to be replicas of
the Dearborn setup, but they devote more time to press agentry
and product publicity. This takes all the standard forms, with
special attention to advertising tie-ins, the loan of company cars
to prominent citizens who are likely to give them "visibility" and
stunts of all kinds.

The report of the New York office for September 1958, summarized a typical month's effort. At the time New York was
publicizing the Consumers' Conference (forty newspaper articles appeared) and rounding up a large assortment of press people—including thirty-two "teenage reporters"—to go to Dearborn
for the annual car preview showings. Some time was also found
to furnish PR assistance to local plants involved in strikes and
contract negotiations. A total of forty-five press releases were
issued during the month.

A major effort was devoted to magazine contact, with a good
deal of material being furnished on Ford products. "Worked
with *Time,*" the report noted, "on providing approved close-up
photo features of 1959 cars in advance of introduction . . .
Worked with *Reader's Digest* on paint research article . . .
Forbes, major article on auto industry . . . *Parents,* major 1959

station wagon article for February issue . . . *Vision,* new Ford robot and cultivator material . . ."

Advertising tie-in efforts resulted in four new placements, bringing New York's total for the year up to forty-two. The new coups included displaying a Lincoln Continental in a Lufthansa Airlines ad and a Ford Country Sedan in a Bethlehem Steel ad; the layouts were scheduled to appear in *Time, Newsweek* and *Business Week,* excellent showcases which in this instance cost Ford nothing. Lufthansa and Bethlehem were obliging, one gathered, because they received the use of the cars at no cost.

Free visibility was sought in all directions. Two office convertibles were promised spots in New York's Columbus Day parade the following month. An Edsel convertible was placed at the disposal of a company making a film on safe driving, scheduled for television showing. "Excellent visibility" of company products was achieved at Newport, R.I. during the America's Cup races, the major success being modestly noted: "Arranged loan of 22 cars complete with R.I. license plates for use by vacationing President Eisenhower . . ."

Somehow there was also time during the month for a bit of community relations ("Handled visit of Harrison Williams, New Jersey Democratic senatorial candidate to Mahwah . . . Arranged three Mahwah plant tours . . .") and several miscellaneous projects, such as placing a Thunderbird trade-mark in a Houghton Mifflin textbook on advertising.

But there was no time in September, apparently, for a stunt. An effective one was carried off in October—solemnized as the 50th Anniversary Model-T Commemorative Program. The idea was to assemble a Model T of 1909 vintage at the Mahwah plant in New Jersey and to compare it with the wonders of Ford's 1959 car. After the ancient vehicle rolled off the line, it raced the 1959 car around a track to see which could go farther on one-tenth of a gallon of gas. To the vast surprise of no one, the new car proved to be more economical. More than sixty reporters and photographers immortalized the event. It was a natural for television.

As stunts go, this one was somewhat sedate. More imaginative was a little venture in Chicago in the middle of an August heat wave. A heavy truck lumbered on to Michigan Avenue one morning and disgorged an Edsel sedan covered from bumper to bumper with two inches of ice (achieved by lodging the vehicle for a day and a half in a commercial freezing plant at twenty degrees below zero). The frozen auto—dubbed the "Edsicle" by Ford's press agents—was promptly surrounded by a platoon of models, photographers and curious passers-by who slowed traffic until the odd thing melted to normal proportions. By the time the afternoon papers hit the streets, all of Chicago learned of the wonder.

The circus press agent who put that midget on J. P. Morgan's knee obviously had nothing to teach Ford.

11

The PR
Campaign

In a less self-conscious era, Edward Bernays could write an article entitled "Manipulating Public Opinion." Today few PR men would avow such an intention, preferring to speak of "public enlightenment" and "educational campaigns." Yet whatever its pejorative overtones, manipulation characterizes most PR campaigns.

To manipulate, according to one of many dictionary definitions, is "to manage artfully or fraudulently." It would be inaccurate to allege fraud in the majority of public relations ventures; but artfulness is present in any campaign of decent competence. The basic artistry relates to the indirection of the effort. Even a campaign that appears straightforward may involve a sophisticated interplay of symbols, emotional language and the vast range of semantic gimmicks designed to endow a piece of special pleading with a seemingly universal appeal. A

PR campaign may make use of logical argument, but it is hardly an effort at dispassionate intellectual persuasion.

There are degrees of manipulation, of course. Dr. Arnold Kauffman of the University of Michigan once defined manipulation in public relations as the situation existing "when both the *source* and *intent* of the propaganda are disguised." This, however, defines an extreme condition, such as the Byoir campaign in behalf of the railroads, where "front" organizations financed by the railroads were set up to issue material blaming the trucking industry for the sad state of the highways. In this case, the source was certainly disguised, and the ultimate intent—to gain a competitive advantage for the railroads—was hardly indicated either.

There are far more innocuous examples of manipulation, of course. A standard operation in product publicity is to insinuate mention of a product in a context where the reader or viewer is unaware that he is being subjected to an advertising plug. Venetian blinds, for example, show up in a television scene or a movie sequence; only a sophisticated viewer would realize that Venetian blinds rather than bamboo shades are shown because some PR type got the jump on the competition; and only the trade would know that Ruder & Finn, Inc. had long been undertaking a promotional effort on behalf of the Venetian Blind Institute of America. In this instance, the intent of the propaganda, if it could be called that, and its source would be veiled from the public, though the show—or at least the prop department—would be well aware of the source of the window coverings.

Indeed, in most PR campaigns the media are usually aware of who is pushing what product, idea or legislative proposal; such information may or may not be passed along to the public, however. Moreover, in an elaborate PR campaign the public is courted in a variety of ways not involving the printed word: through radio and television, the cinema, speeches by leading citizens and a judicious conveyance of word-of-mouth propaganda (standard procedure is to try to reach the public through a community's "opinion-makers").

The very complexity, not to say irrationality, of opinion-formation usually requires of a public relations campaign that it be manipulative at least in the sense of being indirect, subtle and ingenious. (We are talking here only of campaigns, not of the routine informational activities of a corporation, trade union or government press office.) A straightforward, self-serving approach could never make a dent in the public prints. Nothing would be gained, for example, by a company touting its own merits in a series of press releases. Let it endow a scholarship program, or run a symposium on urban redevelopment, or tour a symphony orchestra through the hinterland, and it both "creates news" and spins an aura of agreeable civic spirit—which in turn may help the sale of its product or efface the memory of past indiscretions. The intent of such manipulation may well be innocuous; its by-products may also be a positive boon to the community; but manipulation it remains, nonetheless.

We examine here three typical public relations campaigns, each revealing varied facets of the manipulative skills. One involves a well-financed propaganda drive in behalf of a piece of legislation. One is an imaginative example of a product publicity campaign. The third is a campaign on behalf of a foreign government—an effort to gain wider "visibility" for a national image.

Back in the autumn of 1954, the producers of natural gas

sought the assistance of Hill and Knowlton, Inc. to escape the rigors of federal price regulation, imposed by the Supreme Court in the Phillips decision of June 1954. The Natural Gas and Oil Resources Committee, as the group was called, wanted a PR campaign to arouse the country to the dangers of federal control. (The principal danger, the industry argued, was that price-fixing by the Federal Power Commission would dampen the incentive to further exploration of gas deposits. The opposition, as could be expected, argued that freedom from price control would allow the industry to make unconscionable profits at the expense of the consumer.) The NGORC's goal, of course, was to get legislation enacted reversing the court's decision, but direct lobbying was left to other agencies.

H and K tackled the PR operation with its accustomed thoroughness. All media were used—newspaper and magazine ads, news and editorial columns, radio and TV, printed booklets and a film. Over a seventeen-month period, H and K billed its client for $1,687,706.30. Of this sum, nearly $400,000 went to the PR firm for its retainer and staff charges. The rest was out-of-pocket expenses, of which advertising was the biggest item—almost $800,000. At the height of the campaign, Hill and Knowlton had sixteen employees assigned to the account—a large number, as PR campaigns go.

This was the general staff of the campaign, which masterminded the advertising program, funneled material to national publications, "monitored the press." "Every time an editorial or statement appeared opposing our stand, we would arrange for an answer," says H and K President Bert Goss.

New York headquarters also supervised the operation of a network of local volunteers—mostly drawn from the gas and oil industry—which eventually numbered three thousand. There were regional chairmen in each of fifteen regions, state chairmen in the forty-eight states and the District of Columbia. One of Hill and Knowlton's first moves was to call the regional chairmen to New York for a two-day "indoctrination" session in December 1954. Ways of recruiting volunteers, reaching the local press, TV and radio stations, placing speakers before Chambers of Commerce, service and women's clubs, enlisting the co-operation of allied industries were exhaustively discussed. Each of the regional chairmen was provided with a large loose-leaf dossier, spelling out in detail the mechanics of conducting a public relations campaign in a community. ("Timeliness is all important. A release about a coming event should be delivered at least a day before the event occurs. . . . In contacting women's groups, it is better, where possible, to have a woman make the arrangements. Since many of our wives belong to such organizations as League of Women Voters, investors study groups, alumni chapters, Eastern Star, and veteran's auxiliaries, they might be very helpful in obtaining a hearing before such groups.") Laden with this printed expertise, the regional chairmen then held indoctrination sessions for their state chairmen during January and February 1955.

Meantime, in January, Hill and Knowlton threw a luncheon press conference at New York's Savoy-Plaza for editors of trade publications and reporters from the wire services and financial sections of the New York newspapers. "Shortly thereafter," a later progress report noted, "an industry member of the NGORC staff, accompanied by a representative of public relations counsel, over a period of several weeks visited and briefed the editors of such publications as *Saturday Evening Post, Time, Newsweek, Business Week,* and *Collier's.*"

A nationwide advertising effort was also going forward. Hill and Knowlton had prepared an internal document called "Basic Principles for Advertising Program" which summarized, as well, the underlying strategy of the entire public relations campaign. It was the only internal document, kindly furnished to this writer by H and K, which spoke with any candor about how the highly skilled headquarters team was approaching its mission; many of the other communiqués to staff read like editorials.

At the outset, H and K suggested that its task was difficult because a) "the case is necessarily involved"; b) the Supreme Court ruling lent an aura of authority to the proponents of regulation; c) the proposed reform legislation could be interpreted as "another give-away"; and d) "There is a large segment of the population that is automatically suspicious of anything that is advocated by 'the big companies' or the 'Texas millionaires.'"

The primary audience to be won over consisted of opinion leaders—editors, business and professional men, club leaders; the secondary audience was "consumers and citizens generally (including housewives)." Each of these targets could be divided into three groups: "confirmed 'free-enterprisers,'" who detested any increase in statism, were "instinctively" sympathetic to the gas producers, but had to be "mobilized"; "doctrinaire statists" so set in their ways that no effort should be expended in reaching them; and "independents—those who are open to argument on questions like this." Much of the advertising should be directed at this latter group, though in a fashion not to dismay the free-enterprisers.

Precise directives indicated how this could be done. First of all, "The program should reflect that it is being conducted on behalf of thousands of producers, small and large, and not just by a few 'big companies.' . . . there should be a conscious effort to subordinate the New York headquarters and to reflect the grass roots support for the program." Thus, H and K invariably referred in its material to five thousand producers of natural gas, regarding it as a matter of little consequence that the eight largest firms were responsible for 28 per cent of the natural gas production in the country, and that the eighty largest produced something under 80 per cent of the total output.

At the same time, the considerable expense of the campaign was to be disguised: "The program should be impressive enough to gain widespread attention but not so flamboyant as to make it appear to be backed by limitless resources. This means, for example, that advertising should be prominent enough to stand out but not so large or splashy as to appear lush."

A careful appeal to rational consideration was urged: "To combat charges of 'sneak' and 'give-away,' the program should stress that the public is being invited and urged to examine the issue carefully. This means making repeated use of such phrases as 'The American public is entitled to know the facts' or 'You have a right and an obligation to learn . . .'"

Lest the "independents" be offended, it was also important that the campaign not seem "to square off against the entire Supreme Court of the United States." Wherever possible, the court should not even be mentioned in ads; if it was mentioned, a phrase such as "a 5-to-3 majority of the Supreme Court held" was preferred to "the Supreme Court decided."

The sensibilities of the independents were also to be favored by sparing use of such labels as "socialism" and "bureaucracy," which "have been so abused in past campaigns against everything from Social Security to SEC." Better to tout "free enterprise" than damn "socialism."

Finally, Hill and Knowlton cautioned against a scare campaign: "Americans don't scare easily . . . it is far better to emphasize that free competition is the best way to assure abundance than to say or imply 'we will cut off the supply unless . . .'"

These themes found expression in a vast deluge of speeches, ads, memoranda, press releases, canned editorials. Hill and Knowlton did more than lay down the guiding principles; it showed exactly how they were to be carried out. The direction of its volunteer force of three thousand was a wondrous thing to behold. Nothing was left to chance.

To each of the volunteers, for example, went a fat kit labeled "Materials for Speakers." It contained not only a sheaf of "Background Materials" ("Natural Gas—A Brief Review," "Natural Gas—A Key Resource In Jeopardy," "Some Questions People Are Asking . . .") but also:

Suggestions for Speakers

Two Speeches for Civic and Service Clubs

Speech for Business and Professional Women's Clubs

Speech for General Women's Clubs

Advance and Follow-up Press Material for Each *Speech*

Five-Minute Radio Talk for Local Gas or Oil Industry Man

Five-Minute Radio Talk for Wife of a Gas or Oil Industry Man

Fifteen-Minute Radio Interview for Housewife

Fifteen-Minute Radio Interview for Gas or Oil Industry Representative.

The advance and follow-up press material for *each* speech consisted of press releases that summarized the speaker's remarks, quoted portions of his text, and merely left blanks for the name of speaker, sponsoring organization and so on.

One has an Orwellian image of hundreds of faceless men, on any night of the week, orating to their countrymen in the same phrases, with the same emotional fervor, and having their words immortalized the following day in identical news stories from Florida to Oregon. ("If it is right for the private producer of one basic commodity to be regulated from Washington, then it must be right for all of them to be regulated—other fuels, minerals, agricultural products, steel, timber, anything that is moved in interstate commerce.")

At the same time, hundreds of housewives are sitting before microphones for informal interviews with NGORC militants and announcers. With girlish spontaneity, the housewives express surprise, admiration, awe at the wonders of natural gas— and a proper good citizen's concern about the threat of an ogrish government. ("You know something, Mr. ——, I find this so interesting I'm going to quiz my husband about it this evening. I'll bet *he* doesn't know *anything*—even less than I—because he doesn't do the housekeeping!")

The massive rendition of the cause of free enterprise, as drafted by Hill and Knowlton, proved anything but embarrassing. The speeches, radio interviews, ads and film showings were supplemented, among other things, by an Editor's Information File sent to every daily paper in the country and thousands of weeklies. The kit included the standard background pamphlets as well as two canned editorials, a feature story, photographs and short fillers. ("Twenty-one million residences now use natural gas . . . There are some 5,000 competing producers of natural gas in the United States, according to the Federal Power Commission.") The pay-off, according to one tally, was 1,718 favorable editorials, 538 unfavorable, 210 neutral. The Editor's Information File, of course, deserved only part of the credit; there were also those 3,000 volunteers busy buttonholing editors in their offices.

By September 1955, midway in the campaign, Hill and Knowlton and NGORC could rack up some substantial accomplishments. There had been 6,300 speeches and showings of the film, "You, the People," which was also displayed 230 times on television. The natural gas producers had presented their case on 60 other TV shows as well as on 475 radio broadcasts. A total of 2,400 "contacts" had been made with Chambers of Commerce, 3,400 with daily newspapers, 4,300 with weekly newspapers. Some 5,500,000 pieces of literature had been distributed. Favorable resolutions had been adopted by "more than 120 civic, municipal, Chamber of Commerce, business and industrial organizations in 34 states."

In the end, the bill freeing natural gas producers from price control was passed by the Congress. President Eisenhower, who had favored the legislation, vetoed it for an extraneous reason —because of indications that an effort had been made to influence a senator's vote through a campaign contribution. Neither Hill and Knowlton nor its client had any involvement in this episode.

H and K had done its job. But what played the most important role in passing the bill—the public relations effort or the lobbying campaign? "That's one of the tragedies of PR," says Bert Goss. "At the end of two years we couldn't tell you that we had changed opinions two points or ten points or thirty points."

Late in 1955, Communications Counsellors, Inc., a subsidiary of the McCann-Erickson Advertising Agency, found itself entrusted with an equally difficult mission: to persuade the women of America to buy more hats. Its client was the Millinery Institute of America, which was understandably dismayed that dollar volume of retail sales had declined 7 per cent between 1952 and 1954 and was showing no signs of recovery in 1955.

The first major step of CCI, which is passionately devoted to research, was to launch "extensive market, motivation, and buyer research studies in order to determine first hand and on a sound basis consumer facts and opinions about millinery."

The facts and opinions, to put it mildly, were deplorable. No more than 22 per cent of American females regularly wore hats; 32 per cent seldom or never wore them. Eighteen per cent of the ladies hadn't bought a hat in more than two years; 40 per cent had only bought one during that period.

Even more disturbing was the fact that "The majority of women's feelings towards . . . the 'hat image' are narrow, limited and special." Women tend to associate hats, CCI's surveyors discovered, with formal occasions or with a sophisticated style of life rather than with their casual, everyday existence. In one plaintive paragraph, CCI observed that "Hat conscious women are generally those who have a great deal of free time . . . mature, fashionable, sophisticated, socially active, upper class or professional women—such is not the average American woman who opposes this common stereotype . . ."

In an effort to provide the average woman with a more congenial stereotype, Communications Counsellors' basic strategy was to try to make the hat a part of the landscape of everyday, casual, unsophisticated America. When hats started to appear on models' heads on Coca-Cola billboards, it was a triumph. Every time another Hollywood ingenue, of the girl-next-door variety, was seen in a piece of casual headgear, CCI scored again. Public figures in every walk of life, with whom the hatless multitude might identify, were assiduously cultivated. Even the sophisticated market was not entirely overlooked. The general scheme was to give the hat a contagious "visibility" under all circumstances.

Each year since 1955 (CCI retained the account until April 1959), the program has undergone certain changes in emphasis, of interest only to the specialist; its general flavor can be appreciated if we just examine CCI's efforts during the first five months of 1958.

The period was marked by several achievements, perhaps most noteworthy the emergence of Mrs. Eisenhower, in a fetching hat, on the cover of *The American Weekly*, a Sunday supplement with a circulation of many millions. Mrs. Eisenhower's appearance was part of a series of portraits by artist Jon Whitcomb, which CCI arranged for. There was no partisan flavor to the enterprise, for Mrs. Roosevelt was also included; the other ladies, all attractively "hatted," were Lucille Ball, Kathy Crosby, Marilyn Monroe and Elsa Maxwell—a sufficiently varied assortment to prove that anyone can wear a hat.

Surprisingly, there was no difficulty recruiting Mrs. Eisenhower for this commercial venture. "Mrs. Eisenhower likes hats and has been friendly to us for a long time," Mark Foster, CCI account executive, explained. "We just approached her through her secretary." But Mrs. Eisenhower would not accept the original suggestion that she appear in an Easter bonnet. "She didn't want to be tied down to a spring hat, but the idea of Whitcomb painting distinguished women in bonnets appealed to her."

The mere appeal of a free hat was enough to elicit cooperation from prominent ladies throughout the land. One of CCI's most elaborate projects was a "Salute To Spring" extravaganza in New York City. Each season the city fathers give their blessing to a promotion financed by one or another of New York's industries; it was now millinery's turn. The event started with a parade up Fifth Avenue, featuring horse-drawn carriages with floral decorations and violinists playing Viennese music. A central attraction was a platoon of United Airlines hostesses, decked out in hats bearing the flower or color of each of the forty-eight states.

When the assemblage reached the vicinity of the Plaza Hotel, there was an open-air fashion show, after which Mrs. Robert Wagner, the wife of the mayor, greeted each of the girls. They were each given a letter addressed to the wives of America's forty-eight governors, after which both letters and hats were flown out to the ladies by United Airlines. The governors' wives all obliged by accepting the gifts and posing for photographers. Each step in the promotion was accompanied by extensive publicity—newspaper pictures, radio coverage, newsreel and television sequences. Total cost to the millinery industry was between $1,500 and $2,000. It seemed worth it.

Another spring event, as in past years, was Easter Seal Bonnet Teas in New York and in some twenty-five other cities. This is a three-way "tie-in," in which the Tea Council promotes its product, the Millinery Institute celebrates hats, and the National Society for Crippled Children raises funds through ticket sales. The formula is simple enough: the audience sips tea while various prominent ladies as well as professional models show off the latest millinery. In New York, in 1958, the featured participants were entertainment stars—among them Gwen Verdon, Mindy Carson, Celeste Holm. In previous years, CCI has enticed "diplomatic wives," "ad wives," "cabinet wives" for the Bonnet Teas.

These were all special events. Throughout the period, CCI continued its devoted efforts to get hats seen and mentioned in every medium of communication. Fifty-two TV network shows, for example, ran hat fashion shows or "included favorable hat comments by personalities." Hats got a big boost on the Arthur Godfrey, Dinah Shore, Perry Como, Eddie Fisher, Dave Garroway shows. Art Linkletter's "House Party" ran a hat show; hats were displayed for a full week on the "Today" program.

How are such plugs obtained? "It's done through producer contacts," says Murray Martin, executive CCI vice-president who supervised the millinery account. "A hat show is an entertainment feature of great interest to women." The client pays the expenses of all the models, and frequently gives away hats. When CCI began its labors for the Millinery Institute, it circulated advertising agencies, TV producers, network costume departments, offering hats and millinery know-how for every type of program. A "hat pool" was even established at NBC to service any program with a bareheaded actress.

CCI made a special pitch for the youth market. One project was to get newspaper photographs and a TV spot for "Miss Secretary of 1958," tastefully turned out in one of the latest creations. CCI offered a helping hand to Glamour's "Ten Best Dressed College Girls" promotion, which was duly immortalized on NBC and CBS television programs. Two youthful Hollywood stars were "hatted" for special publicity pictures. A pair of phonograph records—"In That Hat" and "Patti Ann"—were heavily promoted. Each of these songs, subsidized by the milliners, plugged a hat theme. "Patti Ann," celebrating the joys of "going steady," noted helpfully "that a hat suits her just right." "In That Hat" is built around the jolly notion that the hat sparked the romance.

Throughout the campaign, of course, the fashion press was showered with hat publicity, eighteen fashion shows for press and public were held, special "informational kits" on "The Up-swept Look" and "The Hilite Look" were released. Every second month, CCI prepared a "Fashion News Service" for distribution to two thousand fashion editors on daily and weekly papers.

At the same time, a diligent effort was made "to have women seen wearing hats at leading restaurants and supper clubs in New York City and in other cities." The method was simple, though CCI executives are rather shy about explaining it: the agency recruited society girls, dispatched them to various milliners who were delighted to provide free hats so long as the ladies promised to display them in the right places. This in turn provided an opportunity for a hat plug in a society or gossip column. Gossip columnists, of course, were regularly serviced with bulletins by the CCI staff. A typical one, says Mark Foster, "would be that Aly Khan went to the theater and found himself sitting behind Shirley Temple wearing a big hat—and he was too much of a gentleman to ask her to remove it." Such revelations enlivened the columns of Dorothy Kilgallen, Ed Sullivan, Chollie Knickerbocker and several others.

No angle, apparently, was overlooked. As it proudly reported to its client, "CCI personnel assisted McCann-Erickson and other advertising agencies in obtaining hats for inclusion in ads for the following advertisers: Hancock Life Insurance, Andrew Arkin, The Blouse Institute, Cone Mills, Avis Rent-A-Car (even to the degree of assisting in the selection of the official hat for the uniform), Revlon and Lilt commercials on television . . . Dodge automobile tie-ins . . . Tampax, Warner's Foundation Garment." A hat, apparently, can be an accessory for anything.

What had all this done to sell more hats? "The statistics are very inadequate," says Murray Martin. "There are no set of statistics that are accepted by everybody in the industry." The statistics were apparently sufficiently adequate for a CCI report in 1957 to observe that for the first six months of 1956 retail sales had gone up 6 per cent. In the 1957–58 recession sales declined; when the recession lifted, they began to improve. On the other hand, CCI can reasonably argue that without its efforts sales would have declined even more in a period of recession.

Time was when a foreign government could be adequately represented in the United States by an embassy, a string of consulates and perhaps a tourist office. These days, however, a PR counsel in New York—with outposts throughout the country—seems to be as essential to a foreign government as to a manufacturer of breakfast food, steel ingots or hula hoops. The purposes are equally commercial.

Thus, when Communications Counsellors set to work for the Belgium government in 1957, its objectives were to promote the sale of Belgian products in the U.S., attract more American investment to Belgium and, as a CCI report phrased it, generally to "put Belgium on the map"—an aspiration for which several centuries of recorded history were apparently not sufficient.

The techniques of publicizing a country are essentially no different from those involved in celebrating a corporation. A country, however, is usually a more abundant source of exploitable material; it has quainter traditions, a greater range of products and more colorful personalities. Even General Motors, after all, does not boast a royal family. Despite these advantages, Belgium was apparently in desperate need of a public relations program. CCI's voluminous research studies showed that the

American businessman knew little of Belgium's glowing opportunities, and the average citizen was even more oblivious to her charms.

The process of winning esteem and commerce for Belgium was approached through every channel of communication. The business press was cultivated for sobersided stories of Belgian products and investment opportunities; a newsletter of facts and figures was circulated among editors and leading businessmen; feature material was fed to general circulation newspapers and magazines; product publicity was pushed by way of the women's pages, radio and television; a judicious use was made of "created events."

CCI was quick to get into the act whenever Belgium inadvertently found herself in the news. In the early months of the account, Charles Van Doren, the quiz champion, was finally bested on the "21" television program when he failed to name Belgium's King Baudouin. Such was the national mania for quiz programs that Van Doren's defeat became a front-page news story across the country. CCI immediately wangled an invitation for him to visit Belgium as a guest of the Belgium Tourist Bureau, had the announcement on the wires before midnight. There was also a release, "The King Who Dethroned Van Doren," which was widely reprinted. As CCI later reported to its client, the incident gave it the opportunity "to inject into a general story a few hard facts about Belgium industry and commerce with the United States, viz.: 'Belgium is the third largest European supplier of foreign products for the United States.' —'Belgium has taken the lead in exploiting nuclear energy for power in Western Europe,' etc."

Normally, however, Belgium was not fortuitously catapulted into the news. CCI had to sweat for every puff it received; it overlooked few exploitable morsels. For example, the female president of Pepperidge Farm, a bakery using Belgian recipes, visited Brussels to collect more recipes. CCI's Brussels office thereupon put on a "full scale promotion" revolving around her visit to a Brussels bakery, which became the basis for a feature story distributed to U.S. newspapers. Special articles were prepared for bakery magazines in the U.S. CCI went so far as to recommend that the lady receive a decoration for her "contribution to Belgo-American commerce and culture," pointing out that this could generate more publicity.

The suggestion apparently fell on deaf ears, but CCI was more successful with other "special events" to attract attention to Belgian luxury products. General Anthony McAuliffe, the hero of Bastogne, was presented with a pewter tray. A crystal ash tray was bestowed on California Governor Goodwin Knight by a functionary in the San Francisco Belgian consulate. Elizabeth Taylor received a crystal vase, the mayor of St. Louis a copper tray, Governor Harriman a glass plaque bearing the seal of New York State. Each of these ceremonies was duly recorded in the press.

In a mere three-month period, May to July 1957, CCI undertook a bewildering variety of projects. It distributed thirty-eight news and feature stories, "assisted" a *Wall Street Journal* editor researching a piece about atomic energy in Belgium, "co-ordinated" the publicity for Belgium's participation in the San Diego County Fair, got Belgian products described on the Dave Garroway "Today" show, wangled two articles in the business section of the New York *Times* (CCI prepared fifteen thousand words of memoranda to aid the writer), inspired a feature in the Los Angeles *Mirror-News* on Belgium's diamond exports, arranged for a travel story in the New York *World-Telegram and Sun*.

CCI's pursuit of the press was relentless. In the case of the hapless *World-Telegram* man, CCI reported to its client, "The editor was 'followed' from the time he won a free trip to Belgium at an Overseas Press Club dinner until he collected material for an article in Belgium with the assistance of CCI-Brussels."

Nor was this all. That hectic spring, CCI also prepared a "Background Paper on American Investments," which was made use of by the New York *Times* and the *Journal of Commerce*. In Los Angeles, the city council was persuaded to "honor" Belgium National Day, an event which got a big play in the papers. CCI-Los Angeles helpfully prepared the resolution adopted by the city council. CCI's operatives also found time for a little intelligence work. As it later recalled to its clients, "Before Mr. Adlai Stevenson's visit to Belgium, CCI-Brussels was able to notify the proper authorities as to the questions for which Mr. Stevenson would be likely to request information during his interviews with the Foreign Affairs Minister." This service, one gathers, was above and beyond the call of duty.

The PR firm had its problems. As it later complained to its client, it had been "prevented by consular directive from publicizing dramatic use of Belgian structural steel in New York City for fear of arousing the antagonism of New York building trades." Similarly, it was instructed to keep quiet about the exports of Belgian broadloom to the U.S.—lest American carpet manufacturers be spurred to try to obtain a higher tariff.

Despite these frustrations, CCI turned in an energetic performance in 1957. A total of 19,481 man-hours was devoted to the job; staff members covered 38,000 miles in their missionary travels. Among the results were 704 stories in newspapers with a combined circulation of 75,000,000; 145 articles in the technical and trade press; use of canned scripts—largely of a women's interest character—on 1,251 television and 6,906 radio programs.

Only two uncomplimentary stories appeared in the U.S. press during 1957, CCI reported. "One, dealing with defective Belgian-made grenades, supposedly sold to the U.S., died without creating a stir. The second, protesting Belgian taxes on U.S. exports for exhibition purposes at the Brussels Fair, appeared principally in the Chicago *Tribune*, an isolationist daily in the United States." Criticism from that source, one gathered, hardly mattered.

The client was sufficiently impressed with the results to continue the program until the end of March 1959. CCI outlined a variety of new projects for 1958 which, because of budgetary stringencies, were not authorized. They may be worth describing, however, as a random sampling of PR stratagems which are frequently employed on behalf of foreign governments.

CCI proposed, for example, that it exploit the Brussels Fair by what it called "directed publicity." Hill and Knowlton, Inc. were charged with publicizing the fair itself; CCI was not trying to trench on H and K's preserves, but suggested that by judicious cultivation of American correspondents at the fair, it could "inject" into dispatches "generous doses of the kind of information we want to disseminate in the United States about Belgium itself."

Specifically, it proposed that journalists visiting the fair be taken in hand, entertained, furnished with photographers and provided with travel expenses so that they could journey "where they want to go for material—and more important—where *you* want them to go." After CCI's ministrations, a correspondent who was merely interested in seeing the fair might end up by going to Val St. Lambert to do a story on Belgian crystal or to Bruges to examine the lace industry.

To attract business writers, who would normally not be visiting Belgium for the fair, CCI proposed a press junket for twenty-five of the "most important" business and financial journalists. It suggested that Sabena Airlines furnish free transportation, the exposition pick up the tab for food and lodging and the Belgian government defray the rest of the cost. The expense would be well worth while: "It has been CCI's experience that on special trips of this kind the editors concerned usually do feel a sense of obligation . . . and invariably reciprocate with favorable stories and features."

For a relatively trifling sum, its client could also get the advantage of a New York *Times* special supplement devoted to Belgium. As CCI outlined the procedure, "The government concerned buys this supplement for $10,200 (two pages) and, through its public relations counsel, controls what is printed on various aspects of trade, commerce and industry." The supplement would then be expanded to sixteen pages through ads taken by "associated enterprises"—such as Sabena, the Brussels Fair and the Belgian Congo. The supplement, chock-full of "excellent pictures and tightly written stories" would not only enlighten *Times* readers but would then be "merchandised" by way of mailings to "key opinion-makers, U.S. travel agents, and, of course, in quantity to the Belgian consulates." (The only detail left out, the *Times* informed this writer, is that every page of such a supplement would be labeled "Advertisement." Other newspapers are not so finicky.)

Even more important would be a long-range book program. There was a dearth of good books on Belgium, said CCI, and the way to repair the deficiency was to subsidize their production.

It outlined the plan in detail: First you approach the writer, "a recognized leader in his field"; next you work out a story outline—"so that you have some advance assurance of a final result"; then you pay the writer's travel expenses to Belgium and living expenses while he researches his volume. And as the PR firm cagily pointed out, if the writer "is working under a subsidy, CCI has an opportunity to indirectly guide his writing and has the privilege of reviewing the final manuscript to go to the publisher." And all this for an estimated three thousand dollars per book—if Sabena and Belgium's patriotic hotel industry would co-operate with free service or cut rates in return for mention in the book.

A similar plan was suggested for the production of a motion picture on the European common market—which "would be subtle in the treatment of the Belgian image. Obviously, it would span the six countries who have banded together . . . But it would emphasize Brussels as the logical and strongest contender for the Capital of the Common Market . . ." If the Belgian government were to produce this film itself, it would cost $100,000; but if it underwrote the expenses of a regular motion picture company, which would distribute the film and make its normal profit, the government would be out of pocket by no more than $27,000.

Everybody would gain in all these projects—except of course the public, unaware of who was subsidizing whom and for what purpose.

12

The Nonprofit Field

"I am by profession a Methodist minister, but I haven't practiced it for nineteen years." Instead Dr. Ralph Stoody has been practicing the arts of press agentry on behalf of the Methodist Church. Dr. Stoody, a short, rotund and very jolly man, advances no claim to the title of public relations counsel but modestly calls himself a publicity man. He knows many of his bishops by their first names, but hardly suggests that he advises on high policy. He merely tries to get the church a good press. He has been very successful.

The Methodists have hardly been alone in extending their proselytizing efforts to all the media of mass communication. Virtually every major denomination in America has felt compelled to avail itself of the techniques of public relations. So have a variety of other organizations in the nonprofit field—educational institutions, hospitals, health and welfare groups, labor unions and governmental bodies—city, state and federal. Indeed, there has been no area of American life, in the last two decades, where the rationales and methods of public relations have not penetrated.

Daniel Seligman of *Fortune* tells an entertaining little story which illustrates the wide reach of the PR gesture. In 1956 he was preparing an article for his magazine on the ructions besetting the dwindling band of American Communists. He scheduled a luncheon interview with Simon Gerson, who served informally as a Communist party press agent, and they had a meal at a moderately expensive New York restaurant. When the session was over, Gerson reached for the check. Seligman demurred: "But surely you don't have an expense account?" Gerson maintained that he did—and would merely list the item as "Lunch with hireling of the capitalist press." In the end Seligman persuaded him to let the capitalist press pay.

Although the methods of public relations were originally shaped by the needs of business, they have been readily adapted to such diverse purposes as raising funds for hospital construction, rallying public support in a labor negotiation, advancing the cause of the Air Force as against that of the Army, or promoting the sale of Israel bonds. So well developed is PR in the nonprofit field that a number of professional organizations are required to service the various specialities involved—among them the National Religious Publicity Council, with chapters in nine cities around the country; the American College Public Relations Association, which early in 1959 had a membership of 880 colleges and 50 educational agencies and associations; and the National Publicity Council for Health and Welfare Services, Inc., whose constituency during the same period consisted of some 1,900 agencies on the local, state and national levels.

Press agents first went on the federal payroll in the early

years of this century. By the fiscal year 1952, according to a survey of the Budget Bureau, full-time PR employees numbered 2,625.9 and the "full-time equivalent" of part-time employees came to 1,007.5. (The fractional figures because some did not work a full day.) Payroll costs for public relations were more than $17,000,000. Since 1952, there has been no further survey of federal employees engaged in PR work. Statistics on the subject are not very meaningful, however, since many agencies disguise some of their press agents with misleading job titles. The reason is simple: Congress has many times showed its hostility to "propaganda" on the part of executive agencies, fearing that unfair pressure can be brought to bear on the legislative process if the publicity mills grind without restraint.

Outside the world of business, public relations undergoes no profound changes. The shift is largely in the content of the message, not in the means of transmitting it. Occasionally a certain solemnity characterizes the efforts of college or church publicity men, but just as often they promote their product in the uninhibited manner of the entertainment press agent. There are other differences, however. A much larger proportion of public relations activity in the nonprofit field is carried on by staff people than by outside PR firms. The pay is lower and expense accounts more modest than in commercial PR; on the other hand, the job satisfactions are greater—at least to the dedicated. Raising funds for an orphanage or a library somehow seems more worth while than promoting the sale of lingerie or breakfast foods.

As for government public relations, it is many things. An enormous amount of time is devoted to routine and straightforward information work, which is handled by civil servants who remain in office through successive administrations. Personal build-ups for agency heads and efforts to "sell" administration policy to Washington correspondents are usually delegated to political appointees with some such title as "assistant to the secretary." The exception is in the case of the Pentagon, where all three services use military PR personnel in a perpetual battle for a better press and bigger appropriations.

On the highest level, government PR men have a decided advantage over their nongovernmental colleagues. They often have an enormous volume of information at their disposal and are in a position to "manage the news," in James Reston's phrase, in a fashion to benefit their employer's reputation if not always the public interest. The man who sits in the White House press chair has, of course, the greatest managerial opportunities of all. As many observers have noted, when President Eisenhower has gone on a holiday, James Hagerty has often taken along batches of routine announcements and appointments, portions of which he would release each day to give an impression of great Presidential activity.

One of Hagerty's major coups occurred in July 1955, at a time when Secretary of the Air Force Harold E. Talbott was under severe attack and expected momentarily to resign. Hagerty gave advance warning of a major announcement at the White House, and numbers of correspondents assembled, many expecting to hear of Talbott's resignation. Instead they were confronted with a group of scientists and the news that the United States would launch an earth-circling satellite during the International Geophysical Year, due to begin in 1957. This dramatic announcement, which could have been made at any time, blanketed the front pages and obscured the embarrassing Talbott matter. The administration was still suffused in an afterglow of achievement when Talbott's resignation was released three days later.

More than any other phenomenon, the conversion of the churches to public relations indicates that there is no area of American life where the citizen is safe from the intrusion of the mass persuaders. Church PR men argue that the fault, if there be any, lies not in any blunted sensitivity on their part but in the domination of our culture by an enormous apparatus of communication. There is no effective way of reaching the "unchurched" or reassuring the faithful without adding to the general din. Pulpit oratory and pastoral rounds are no longer enough. Bishop Sheen and Norman Vincent Peale take to television, and Billy Graham holds revival meetings in Madison Square Garden. These days the message must be writ large. Any incongruity between the spiritual goals and the exuberantly commercial means is of little consequence. So runs the rationale.

There are, of course, different styles in church public relations. The National Council of the Churches of Christ runs a very dignified operation. With a staff of ten and a budget for 1959 of $149,230, the council's PR office issues a monthly magazine, a weekly mimeographed newsletter, puts out releases and is a vast storehouse of information for reporters who telephone with queries. A separate broadcasting and film division handles those media. The National Council, which represents thirty-three Protestant churches, has so broad a field of interest and generates so much legitimate news in the normal course of business that there is no difficulty getting a good play in the press. Energetic press agentry is not needed. In the view of Donald Bolles, who headed the operation until May 1959, church PR differs from the commercial brand in that "we don't try to pressure anyone." Otherwise, "the techniques are bound to be the same, because the channels of communication—whether they tell about sin or heaven—are pretty much the same. What we're saying is that the media are more and more bothering about heaven. The news about religion in the last decade has moved from the obit page to the front page."

Individual denominations are in a somewhat different position. They have to compete, often strenuously, for attention. In 1958, Helen Smith, who handles publicity for the Seventh-day Adventists in New York, carried off a publicity coup worthy of any of the Broadway press agents whose offices are within a stone's throw of hers on West 46th Street. The occasion was the visit to the United States of Parkin Christian of Pitcairn Island, a descendant of Fletcher Christian, who led the mutiny on the *Bounty*. The Pitcairn Islanders have for many years been Adventists, and seventy-three-year-old Parkin was on his way to the forty-eighth world conference of the church in Cleveland. With so legendary a background, his presence in New York was obviously a very marketable item.

Before his arrival, there was a three-page memorandum to all media on Parkin, the history of Pitcairn and some facts and figures on the Seventh-day Adventists. A few days later came notice of a press conference and Christian's itinerary in New York. The press interviewed him after he landed at Idlewild. A film of his arrival was shown on television. A representative of Mayor Wagner showed him New York from the top of the Empire State Building. Christian appeared on Garry Moore's TV show, "I've Got a Secret." Helen Smith placed him on two or three radio shows. He opened an exhibit at the Adventist center in Manhattan of "rare objects and photos" from the *Bounty* and Pitcairn, took a trip on the Staten Island ferry, journeyed to Mystic, Connecticut, to see an old whaling ship on which his great uncle once sailed. No angle was overlooked and the press was very generous.

"Created events," of course, are only part of a rounded PR program for a church. The Methodist operation of Ralph Stoody is a good example of the fully articulated publicity effort. The church established its Commission on Public Information (now the Commission on Public Relations and Methodist Information) in 1940, with an annual appropriation of $25,000. Stoody, who had served as a pastor for many years and written a doctoral dissertation on the history of religious journalism, was selected to head the new department because, as he modestly puts it, "A minister would work for less than a layman. Initially there was also a certain fear of 'a press agent job,' and it was felt it would be much better to have someone whose first interest would be the church and its welfare rather than getting lots of column inches."

In the ensuing years, of course, Stoody has obtained miles of column mention. By 1959 his appropriation had been increased to $110,000 a year, and he headed a staff of nine people, with a main office in New York and branches in Washington, Chicago and Nashville. In addition, there were twenty other publicity offices in episcopal centers around the country, usually staffed by ex-newspapermen and financed locally, with a small subsidy from the national commission. The Methodist Board of Missions also has long had its own news bureau. As church publicity operations go, this one is substantial.

Stoody and staff push the Methodist story through every available channel. They provide pressrooms at every church-wide conference, issue a continual stream of news releases, produce articles on Methodism for encyclopedias, suggest story ideas to national magazines and even keep tabs on the old college fra-

ternities of Methodist leaders. Whenever a Methodist church-
man or layman wins some honor, copy and photos are promptly
dispatched to his fraternity magazine. As Dr. Stoody cautiously
observed in a report to church leaders in 1952, ". . . the Commission has made little effort to advertise either the nature or
extent of its own operations. This is on the belief that the best
publicity is that which is least recognizable as such. While now
and then news stories or articles appear under the by-lines of
staff personnel, for every such instance there are hundreds of
columns written, suggested, arranged for, supplemented, co-
authored or illustrated by members of the staff, none of which
carry any indication of origin in or relationship to Methodist
Information."

One such instance, of which Stoody is very proud, occurred
in 1947 when the Miss America title was bestowed on twenty-
one-year-old Barbara Jo Walker, who happened to be a Methodist. Stoody, eager to publicize a forthcoming church youth
conference in Cleveland, sprung into action. Through an intermediary, he interested *Look* in doing a picture story of Barbara Jo attending the conference; it was an interesting switch
on traditional Miss America "art." The next problem was to get
her to attend. The young lady, it developed, had never heard
of the Commission on Public Information. Stoody thereupon
telephoned her bishop, who applied the necessary moral sua-
sion. The final result was a pleasant layout in the magazine,
showing Miss Walker at the general session of the conference,
distributing autographs to admirers, folk dancing, and convers-
ing earnestly with Bishop Paul B. Kern. The bishop himself
could hardly have written a more uplifting message to the youth
of America.

On another occasion, *Look* ran an article by Cardinal Spellman on "The Pope's War on Communism." Stoody immediately saw another opening. "We didn't want to leave any false impressions in the minds of the public. So I went to *Look* and asked whether they'd like to have an article on how Protestants were fighting communism." How could *Look* say no? Stoody arranged for Bishop G. Bromley Oxnam to do the piece.

After publication of a favorable article, Stoody usually distributes reprints by the thousands and otherwise promotes it energetically. A few years ago, however, an article in *True Confessions* gave him quite a turn. It was an eminently respectable piece entitled "The Church of Evangelism . . . The Methodists" but *True Confessions* was hardly the sort of magazine which sat well with his constituents. "You can imagine the problem we had with that picture on the cover!" Stoody exclaims. Every impulse of the publicity man suggested that the article deserved "merchandising," but Stoody restrained himself and let the project die in his files.

He allows few opportunities to escape him. A quick perusal of Stoody's release file suggests a relentless exploitation of every Methodist nugget in the news. Thus when J. Ernest Wilkins resigned as an Assistant Secretary of Labor, in 1958, Stoody's Washington office put out a release on Wilkins' elaborate Methodist background, which did seem a bit irrelevant. When President Eisenhower announced committee appointments for the 1960 White House Conference on Children and Youth, Stoody's staff immediately issued a release announcing that "Two Methodist laymen are among the leaders named by President Eisenhower." The Methodist Board of Temperance, which Stoody also services, continually bobs up with announcements in its own area of competence. "It's easier to buy a bottle of beer or whiskey than to find a church," the board reported dolefully at one point

in 1958, "Today there are 131,040 more alcoholic beverage out-
lets in the United States than the combined total of churches,
synagogues and temples." Further dismaying statistics followed,
but to make the release seem less one-sided to newspaper editors, Stoody's Washington office astutely added a couple of paragraphs about an Episcopal clergyman who had suggested that
barkeepers and tavern owners join the church and "quit being
ashamed and embarrassed by your business." Thus endowed
with objectivity, the release had a better chance of being
printed.

Stoody also issues a mat service for small-town papers, which
are presumably so hungry for ready-made material that they
will print anything which has the slightest fillip of interest for
their readers. The mats contain news stories, picture layouts,
feature material, cartoon spreads about the history of Methodism
in the style popularized by Ripley's "Believe It or Not." Virtually all of the material has an obvious Methodist import, but
occasionally an item of broader scope is included. Such was
a chart on the "Religious Affiliation of Congressmen," which
graphically contrasted the numbers of Methodists, Catholics,
Presbyterians, Baptists, Episcopalians, Congregationalists, Dis-
ciples of Christ, Lutherans and others in both the Senate and
House of Representatives. The point was not made explicitly,
but a quick perusal of the chart indicated that Protestants of all
denominations far outnumbered Catholics. That suggestion, it
turned out, was the sole purpose of the item. "This was probably a low-down thing to do," Stoody suggested amiably as he
pointed to the chart in his scrapbook. "We just wanted to get
over the idea that this was still predominantly a Protestant
country. It certainly is, but it often seems to Protestants that
Catholic news is overplayed. The reason is quite understand-

able, of course—New York, Chicago, etc., have large Catholic populations, and the smaller papers tend to follow the lead of the big city papers. I wouldn't want you to get the idea we're anti-Catholic, however. We just want things presented in their right proportions."

To further this effort, the Reverend Stoody relies not merely on Methodist's full-time PR staff around the country. Every year seminars are held to initiate working pastors in the mysteries of public relations. They are instructed about such matters as deadlines, the preparation of news releases and the proper diplomacy in calling upon newspaper editors. Dr. Stoody's stock lecture is "How To Create News When There Is None."

Health and welfare organizations and "cause" groups tend to devote more effort to public relations than do religious bodies. Promotional activities are not an adjunct to their normal functions but often a necessary condition for growth or even for survival. With ever more numerous claimants for the charity dollar, increasing reliance is placed on the most sophisticated techniques of communications to win public support. Fund raising is not the only goal; there is often equal need to encourage community participation in programs, gain acceptance for new ideas and in some cases obtain the support of government bodies.

Sidney Marks, National Secretary of the Zionist Organization of America, goes so far as to characterize his organization as "essentially a public relations operation." ZOA is devoted to promoting the cause of Israel and is also concerned with the cultural and community life of American Jews. It has 184,000 members, a staff of 100 and a budget of $1,250,000, about 70 per cent of which is allocated for use in this country and the remainder in Israel. Most of its activities are directed toward communications. There is a department of public information, which includes a press office and a director of Yiddish publicity; a department of world Zionist affairs, which maintains liaison with Zionist organizations in other countries, sets up conferences in the western hemisphere and issues the Zionist Information Service; a department to promote the sale of Israel bonds; another to promote tourism in Israel; others concerned with raising funds, recruiting new members, stimulating an interest in the Hebrew language and sundry other matters.

The organization also issues a monthly publication, the *American Zionist*, a semimonthly news bulletin and an extensive pamphlet series. "The nature of our organization is such," says Marks, "that every member is bombarded with information so that he necessarily becomes a public relations arm." These bombarded arms then go to work in their communities, spreading ZOA's message to service clubs, church groups and friendly newspaper editors. At a time of crisis, such as occurred when Israel invaded Egypt in 1956, ZOA can mobilize its apparatus with great speed. Soon after the invasion, ZOA played a taped message over a telephone circuit to local leaders in twenty-five communities; this gave them "the line." Frequent press conferences were held, at which a raft of background materials was distributed. Publication of the *American Zionist* was stepped up to three times a month. Special pamphlets were issued, special forums arranged around the country. "The State Department," Marks explains, "says that foreign policy is decided by public opinion—and we try to help formulate that opinion."

In a sense, the American Cancer Society has less ambitious aims than trying to shape American foreign policy. While its ultimate aim is to eradicate cancer, its immediate goals are more susceptible to the ministrations of public relations: educating people to avail themselves in time of what cancer therapies already exist and simultaneously persuading them to contribute to the society's support. Huge sums of money are involved. In 1958, for example, ACS raised approximately $29,700,000, more than double its income ten years before. Contributions of that magnitude would seem to justify the $700,075 which the society budgeted in 1959 for its public education and information department, which is directed by vice-president Clifton R. Read.

In many ways, Read's operation resembles that of a PR department in a large corporation. He has a full-time staff of sixty-eight, divided functionally into units dealing with press relations; films, radio and TV; pictures, ads and exhibits; public education; publications; and production. The headquarters staff deals with the national media and provides detailed guidance to volunteer publicity committees in local units. An enormous volume of free materials—flyers, booklets, publications and films—are distributed around the country. In 1958, for example, the society was turning out printed materials at the rate of 150,000,-000 pieces a year. There is the same stress as in corporate PR on projecting an institutional image, the same concern with such seemingly minor details as promoting the society symbol—an unsheathed sword with two coiled snakes at its base. In a report on his department's 1957–58 activities, Read pointed out that "Important in establishing 'product identity' has been the Graphics section and the uniform quality of design of materials. An institutional film has been in the works and will be ready by the Annual Meeting or soon thereafter."

Like many corporations, the society has a problem with rivals seeking to woo away its customers. In 1958, Read reported, "A sudden flowering in publicity of agencies fighting leukemia—cancer of the blood—led the Society . . . to emphasize its own role in research in leukemia and to make clear its conviction that the most effective way to fight this form of cancer is to support the American Cancer Society."

A more serious institutional embarrassment was the long smoldering controversy between the society and the United Community Funds around the country. In 1957, ACS ordered its local units to sever ties with the United Funds by April 1960. This directive caused considerable resentment among partisans of the United Fund movement, who have long been critical of the duplicated effort and expense of the many competing national health drives. A number of ACS stalwarts in the hinterland were equally resentful. The society insisted, however, that in the long run it would raise more money by going it alone and that an independent drive allowed it to further its educational program while simultaneously collecting funds. Despite these arguments, the society was the recipient of much unfavorable publicity. "Savagely critical editorials," Read reported, "appeared in a number of communities where we are in United Funds and our Crusade identity has not been maintained." (The Crusade is the annual fund drive.) His job, as he saw it, was to keep his principals from replying with equal savagery; any heightening of the controversy would only make matters worse. It was the temperate prescription typical of corporation PR.

In other ways, however, public relations for an organization like the American Cancer Society is a good deal easier than promoting the cause of an oil company or a boiler manufacturer. There is an initial predisposition on the part of the public toward the goals of the society and a gratifying willingness of the media to provide free advertising space as well as favorable editorial mention. The ACS has long made it a policy not to pay for advertisements in the press or on radio or television. Nor would it seem necessary. In 1948, when it began its advertising program, its copy was carried by 409 magazines with a combined circulation of 86,571,000. Ten years later it was receiving free space from 2,861 magazines whose total circulation was 887,232,368. As for television, in the single month of April 1958, an estimated audience of some 400,000,000 viewed "spots" for the 1958 Crusade.

Editorial coverage was equally impressive. Magazines which in 1958 availed themselves of society materials or assistance had a combined circulation of 110,000,000; newspapers, a combined circulation of 764,000,000. The society's publicity efforts were aided, of course, by the fact that its "product" was a broad one: any copy that dealt with cancer—diagnosis, therapy, research efforts, warnings against quackery—aided the cause. Nonetheless, such extensive coverage required continued salesmanship from Read's staff. The magazine section, for example, claimed credit for inspiring articles which appeared from 1956 to 1959 in the *Saturday Evening Post, Life, Reader's Digest, Ladies' Home Journal, Redbook* and other mass-circulation magazines. A special effort was also made to enlighten "the lower socio-economic groups," as Read's report puts it, by reaching such magazines as *True Story* and *True Confessions*. As it moves down the economic scale, the ACS has always had more difficulty arousing people to the dangers of cancer.

In seeking publicity in the daily press, the society has not been content with a routine flow of news releases and story ideas to science and medical writers. It has also managed to adapt the techniques of the junket and the stunt to its own specialized purposes. In 1958, for example, it received an enormous amount of press, radio and television attention by shepherding 40 science writers on a 19-day, 7,000-mile tour of 41 institutions where cancer research was going on; a total of 170 scientists were interviewed. As Read was later able to report: "For 20 successive days, from March 24 to April 13, the nation's wires carried stories about ACS-sponsored research—many of them on page one." This exposure was well worth the expense of transportation and lodging for the junketing reporters. In 1959, the pattern was varied by holding a week-long series of panel discussions on cancer research at Excelsior, Maryland. This time the reporters were kept in one spot and the scientists were transported from all over the country to meet them.

One of the most successful stunts which the society carried off was the Cured Cancer Congress, held in Washington in 1958 and again in 1959 to launch the annual Crusades. A nationwide assemblage of men, women and children who had been cured of cancer could hardly fail to stir sympathy and interest among people indifferent to the latest scientific communiqué. The picture possibilities alone were enormous and coverage—press, radio and television—was very extensive in both 1958 and 1959. The Congress was a good illustration as well of ACS's general educational approach, best characterized as "conservative hope." Strident fear campaigns, it has long believed, only lead people to turn away in an effort to suppress their anxieties. "The way to influence people to go to the doctor or to donate money is to give them hope, to accentuate the positive," says Read. It seems to work.

Trade unions have long been in the business of inspiring hope as well as engendering rebellion but the labor movement has on the whole been laggard in organizing its public relations in any formal manner. The traditional "business unionist," in the era prior to the organization of the mass production industries in the thirties, was often as indifferent to public opinion as was the employer with whom he dealt. The goal of the labor movement, in his view, was summed up by Samuel Gompers' succinct phrase—"More"—and the means was the application of economic strength at pressure points at which the employer was most sensitive. In strikes, assistance might be solicited from other unions, but only infrequently—and generally only in the case of a few broad-visioned unions—from the public at large.

Economic power is still the labor union's basic weapon, but ever since the New Deal increasing effort has been turned to winning public favor. The Roosevelt era showed that labor had much to gain from favorable legislation; political power began to supplement economic power and the former could hardly be consolidated without allies. Moreover, the CIO experience indicated the value of broad community support when the unions embarked on major organizing drives. The new crop of leaders which emerged in the thirties also had a more sophisticated notion of their role in society and an eagerness to perform on a larger platform than that provided by the union hall. Finally, the postwar threat of restrictive legislation, culminating in the passage of the Taft-Hartley Act in 1947, proved that an unfavorable shift in the climate of opinion could have painful effects.

Nonetheless, a consciousness of the value of public relations has not led to the establishment of elaborate PR departments, as has been the case with corporations. The reason is fairly simple. The average industrial leader is a parochial figure, expert in his own specialty, but often at a loss when he has to deal with the mass of his employees or the public at large. He requires labor relations experts to deal with labor, PR experts to deal with the public, speech writers and voice coaches to prepare him for a rare experience on the podium. The labor leader, by contrast, is essentially a political animal; he has won power by being able to sway minds and pyramid loyalties—first in the local union hall and then in the larger arena; his readiest talent is the ability to deliver a speech; and he usually learns early in his career how to handle reporters. They have been around since he ran his first strike. Not every labor leader, of course, is adept in his public role. In the building trades and in the teamsters' union, there are a good many leaders who still operate according to the canons of 1910. Yet the most talented of our labor leaders, up and down the union hierarchy, are essentially their own public relations men; hence they do not require large staffs.

It is difficult to think of Walter Reuther and David Dubinsky, to take two obvious examples, holding up a public gesture until they have the counsel of their PR men. Dubinsky has shown an effortless ability to attract public favor to his union ever since he became president of the International Ladies' Garment Workers in the early thirties. Walter Reuther, long before he was elected president of the auto workers, promoted himself into national prominence by an amazing flair for self-dramatization. From the moment in 1941 when he announced the first Reuther Plan—to convert auto factories to airplane production—his whole career can be regarded as an exercise in public relations.

This concern for public opinion has not prevented certain obvious blunders, however. An incredible *gaffe* came to public attention in 1958, when action by the National Labor Relations Board was required to force the AFL-CIO to recognize the Field Representatives Federation, a union of its own organizers. The persistent refusal of our labor chieftains to bargain with their own employees elicited derisive comment throughout the country. The reaction could have been predicted. An equally unflattering press was accorded the sessions of the AFL-CIO executive council at the lush Caribe Hilton Hotel in San Juan,

Puerto Rico, in February 1959. *Life,* for example, ran a picture spread of labor leaders frolicking in the sun while their resolutions solemnly deplored the plight of the unemployed on the mainland. But then the corporations make PR blunders too.

As an organized function in the unions, public relations is kept to modest dimensions. The PR department in the United Automobile Workers is one of the largest in the country, and yet it only consists of three "professionals" and three secretaries. During the course of 1958, the department spent $112,777.56. "Our work is mostly an informational service," says director Frank Winn. "We believe that the best sort of propaganda is propaganda of the deed rather than the word, but we don't go in for gimmicks or stunts." As an example of the deed, Winn mentioned Reuther's widely publicized proposal to the auto companies in August 1957 that they reduce the wholesale price of cars by an average of $100 each, in return for which the union would consider moderating its bargaining demands. To uncommitted observers, this was a pure PR gesture—and a highly successful one—but Winn insists that the union was serious.

Public relations in the UAW is not merely a matter of the PR department. The activities of the education, citizenship, community relations and a few other departments impinge from time to time on public relations. Considerable money is also spent in maintaining regular contact with the union's own members. In 1958, for example, the publications department spent $1,112,128.57, largely to produce the union paper, *Solidarity,* which appeared for the first five months as a weekly and the rest of the year as a bi-weekly. In January 1959 the paper was reduced to monthly appearances at an anticipated annual saving of $400,000. Retrenchment was necessitated because of a drop in dues payments due to heavy unemployment.

A union paper, of course, is a long-established tradition, but the UAW has shown greater enterprise than many other unions by financing two daily radio shows and a weekly television program. In 1958 more than $616,000 was spent on these ventures, and some $200,000 less in 1959. The radio shows are presented early in the morning and in the middle of the afternoon, around the time of shift changes when members are driving to and from work. The morning program, "Eye Opener," is heard in industrial cities around the country; the other is presented only in Detroit, as is the TV discussion show. Both radio programs are a conglomeration of news, interviews, popular songs, jokes and the standard disc jockey patter heavily flavored by the union line. They apparently have a devoted audience of men who cannot drive without a radio blaring in their ears. All in all this represents a more ambitious public relations effort than most unions can boast of and yet it can hardly compare with the year-round campaigns of Ford or General Motors.

When a labor organization attempts an expanded program, it inevitably resembles a corporate PR effort. There are just so many available techniques, one gathers, and the corporations used them first. Thus the steelworkers' union, in preparation for contract talks with the industry which began in May 1959, engaged in an undeclared advertising battle with the American Iron and Steel Institute. The institute published a series of newspaper ads throughout the country arguing that "Inflation robs us all" and the way to prevent inflation was by restraining wage increases. The steel union argued, in turn, that expanding purchasing power was necessary to keep the economy buoyant. A small fortune was spent on this message; to what extent it enhanced the union's bargaining power is the great question.

The AFL-CIO authorized an enlarged PR effort in May 1958;

it too follows the business pattern. For years the National Association of Manufacturers has provided TV stations around the country with a program, "Industry on Parade," which each week celebrates the exploits of a particular company or industry. Now the AFL-CIO is producing a similar series called "Americans At Work," which also covers many industries but with the focus on the man at the bench. Eighty-five TV stations carry the show, which is budgeted at $300,000 a year.

In addition, the AFL-CIO sponsors two daily news programs ($400,000 a year), one with Edward Morgan and the other with John Vandercook; it runs the labor side of a weekly labor-management show on the ABC network; and it distributes a recorded program of interviews with government figures called "Washington Reports To The People." In May 1959, 261 radio stations were broadcasting the program. Another innovation in 1958 was a speakers bureau and a master mailing list to provide an elaborate index to "opinion molders" around the country who are interested in receiving the various specialist publications which the AFL-CIO turns out. The entire program is administered by seven "professionals" and four secretaries. Al Zack, PR director, and his deputy write all the press releases coming out of Washington and arrange all the press conferences. The highest salary in the department is Zack's—a mere $265 a week. Nonprofit PR is dedicated work.

13

Ethics

For many years Edward L. Bernays has proposed that PR men be licensed by the states—in order to elevate standards and exclude charlatans. "The great danger today in our field," says Bernays, "is the operation of a kind of Gresham's Law—bad practitioners driving out the good." The alarm is hardly general, however, and few of Bernays' colleagues echo his call for licensing laws. His proposal is generally regarded as impractical, though highly attractive; many PR men, after all, aspire to the professional status of a doctor or a lawyer.

Within PR ranks, one encounters much protestation about the ethics of the calling. The concern sometimes seems more rhetorical than real. The Public Relations Society of America, for example, has a succinct code of ethics, which, among other things, pledges:

"We will keep our objectives in full accord with the public welfare as well as the interests of our clients or employers.

"We will be guided in all our activities by the standards of accuracy, truth and good taste.

"We will co-operate with fellow practitioners in curbing malpractice."

And yet, paradoxically, the Public Relations Society was not moved to censure perhaps the most flamboyant display of dubious public relations practice in recent years—the performance of Carl Byoir & Associates, Inc., on behalf of the Eastern Railroad Presidents' Conference, in setting up dummy organizations to disguise the source of its propaganda. A move to censure Byoir would hardly be called for, according to Shirley D. Smith, executive director of PRSA, because the case is still *sub judice* —an appeal has been taken. But Mr. Smith somehow misses the point. The issue is not whether the Byoir office violated the law but whether its admitted practice of setting up "fronts" constituted ethical PR behavior. One must sadly conclude that only a doughty moralist, within the PR fraternity, would want to challenge publicly one of the two largest firms in the business.

It would be unfair to suggest, however, that PR practitioners are bereft of ethical scruples. Though it is loath to move against Byoir, the Public Relations Society has a committee at work revising and expanding its code of ethics. And throughout the trade, the well-publicized trucker-railroad litigation in Philadelphia has caused a flurry of head-wagging over the question of the "third party technique."

"When is a 'front' not a 'front?'" was one of the questions at a special session for counselors at the PRSA convention in New York City in 1958. The same issue was explored at length in an article by Edwin C. Kepler in the magazine *PR*, in its July 1958 issue. In Kepler's view, some practices were clearly unethical— such as setting up organizations with fictitious memberships or "having hirelings pose as 'disinterested parties.'" On the other hand, securing the co-operation of legitimate organizations, which champion one's cause out of some bond of common interest, was clearly legitimate.

Between these extremes, Kepler saw a murky and perplexing area. "What about an instance," he wrote, "in which you reactivate a defunct organization, building up its membership, furnishing it with funds, and employing it for your ends? What about a case in which a group of like-minded people voluntarily form an organization at your behest, a bona fide membership organization, but one that operates under your direction, with your funds, solely to advance your mutual cause? What about the case of a recognized expert in a particular field who agrees to speak in his own name on behalf of your cause if you pay his expenses? Should disclosure of your role be required in these instances?"

The unsophisticated layman might well think so. But Kepler, the PR professional, found it difficult to generalize about these hypothetical cases. Instead, he suggested that the ethical question depended on the practitioner's intent and he proposed a pragmatic test: would the PR man or his client be embarrassed if his behind-the-scenes activity were to be revealed in the newspapers? "Prudence, if not conscience, ought to warn a practitioner away from any activity failing that test." But if prudence is the guide, one must cynically ask, would not a practitioner also be justified in weighing the likelihood of exposure against the undoubted advantages of deception?

Most public relations men are embarrassed to air such subjects in public. What ethical discussion does go on usually has the quality of ritualistic incantation—a wearisome process of trying to brush aside criticism by reiterating the nobility of pub-

lic relations' presumed goals. One of the few candid explorations
of the ethical dilemmas of public relations has been provided
by the firm of Ruder & Finn, which has held both staff seminars
and a public conference on the subject.

The Ruder & Finn deliberations, to which brief reference was
made in a previous chapter, were touched with a solemnity
which verged at times on the comic; it seemed doubtful that
many of the problems surveyed required such painstaking analy-
sis before a solution emerged. And yet the R & F discussions,
begun in 1957, are helpful in indicating some of the areas that
trouble conscientious PR men.

One problem propounded at the staff sessions concerned a
client who sold to discount houses but preferred to keep the fact
from the public. Should Ruder & Finn lie on behalf of its client?
The question gave the boys quite a turn. Initially, the minutes
of the meeting indicated, there was a feeling that "our obligation to our client would force us to tell a lie unless we would
hurt our client's business." Dr. Louis Finkelstein of the Jewish
Theological Seminary, present as an observer, thereupon prudently pointed out—as the minutes paraphrased his remarks—
"that we have an obligation not only to [this client] but to all
our clients. If we do tell a lie, it would hurt our own credibility
and therefore hurt in the end all our clients."

A cynic spoke up to suggest "that we usually lie when we are
sure we will get away with it and the reporters won't find out."
A discussion then ensued about the various kinds of lying people
indulge in. This interlude did not seem very helpful in advancing a solution, and practicality kept intruding. "In the long run,"
the minutes suggested, "it is impractical to tell a lie—we can't get
away with it." At this point, Dr. Richard McKeon of the University of Chicago invoked the authority of Immanuel Kant and

started to differentiate between categorical and pragmatic imperatives. The concrete suggestion which emerged was that Ruder & Finn's client be advised either to: a) live up to its policy of not selling to discount houses or b) not lie about it or c) lie itself but not expect Ruder & Finn to lie in its behalf.

On another occasion the problem was whether R & F should publicize a research project which was "fixed" to the decided advantage of its client. The thought was offered that this sort of thing goes on all the time. Moreover, at times "portions of the truth must be hidden in terms of eventual public good." On the other hand, there was the disturbing apprehension that the faked research project might later be exposed. It occurred to the conferees, as well, that "our own honesty is fundamental in the degree of comfort with which we can practice our profession . . . we shouldn't fool ourselves . . ." Certain platonic dialogues then came in for discussion. And finally a prudent solution emerged: that the client be advised to underwrite an honest research project in order to validate the conclusions of the faked one.

It is doubtless true that many PR operators would hardly be troubled by the restraints which conscience, Kant, Plato and Dr. Louis Finkelstein impose on Ruder & Finn. R & F, however, found the experience so stimulating that in October 1958 it sponsored a public symposium which discussed many of the same themes—a three-day conference, at the New School For Social Research, on the general subject of "The Concept of Responsibility in Public Relations." Participants included R & F staff members, part-time representatives from thirty-five U.S. cities and fifteen foreign countries, and several academicians. The press was also invited.

Round tables addressed themselves to such topics as the

"Ethics of Influencing People," "The Conflict between Public Service and Private Interest" and "Public Relations and the Good Society: An Anti-Democratic Force?" The sessions were remarkable for the frank confessional spirit of the participants and for the revealing light shed on the actual practices of public relations, as contrasted with the textbook maxims.

David Finn, for one, sadly conceded that "We conceal facts as public relations people, there is no doubt about it." Often the PR man, he suggested, tries to persuade the client to be more candid in a press release or a photograph, but the client's reluctance is all too likely to prevail. As a consequence, "We take a picture of a product and we dress it up, we retouch it; so it is a phony, it doesn't show the truth about the product. We know the editor isn't going to like it . . . So we are constantly exposed to a kind of chastening from the third parties." It was his view that such editorial chastening was a good thing.

Finn's colleagues were equally unrestrained in deploring their own influence. Harry Hunter commented, "We can get almost anything in the newspapers and magazines distorted, left out, omitted. It isn't checked, it isn't gone into. It is a rather alarming thing." But in his view the fault lay with the press.

Al Eisen was dismayed at how easily fake expertise could be manufactured. "We know that we can always find an 'expert' who will have just the opinion we are looking for that will be in the interest of our client. I refer to a psychologist, a medical laboratory, or what have you. There is nothing that is sacred. There is no place that is safe from the efforts of the public relations man to get some doctor or Professor So-and-so to say what we want said to give validity to our client's point of view."

"So often we have said at the end of a long, hard day," Richard Weiner reflected, " 'We're just prostitutes, we're liars, we're willing to do anything as long as it is legal.' And, let's face it, we can talk all we want about democracy and ethics but when it comes time to getting that clipping in the paper we will make up stories and we'll do the same thing as the charlatans and the only thing is we don't want to admit it except in the privacy of our homes." On the other hand, Weiner offered the consoling thought that "I don't think we are as bad as even we sometimes think we are, and certainly I don't think we are as bad as we could be without the benefit of the democratic process . . ."

A number of concrete problems troubled the conferees. Among them were the standards to be used in accepting clients. Norman Weissman of R & F told of the case of a prospective client who had aroused considerable resentment around the country because of the high pressure tactics and fraudulent claims of his door-to-door salesmen. The situation had deteriorated to the point where the company was losing business. Finally, the company president approached Ruder & Finn with the plea to "Get us out of this mess! . . . Tell the public how good we are so they will believe in us and help us get back the business we have lost!"

Ruder & Finn, however, were not persuaded of the propriety of a simple whitewash job. They toyed with the notion of turning down the company, then accepted it with the provision that it mend its ways. The president agreed, the public relations effort was launched, but the expected reformation did not occur. The president thereupon counseled patience, arguing that it took time to overturn long-established organizational practices. And R & F found itself trapped into doing the very job it had initially declined—"puffing up the client's products and giving currency to some basic untruths." The questions for the class were: could R & F ethically continue the relationship on the assurance that the client would ultimately reform; should it have initially accepted the client; or "should we have forgotten all this 'ethics talk' in the first place, and instead depended on the sifting process of the press, to separate truth from fiction?"

The discussion was lively. Dr. F. Ernest Johnson, of the National Council of the Churches of Christ, thought R & F's initial decision had been correct: a PR consultant had to have a "reciprocal relationship" with a client. Al Eisen was of a similar view, "assuming . . . that the agency in question is in a sound condition and will not live or die on the basis of this one account, in which case all bets are off." But Eisen's reasons for not accepting such a client unconditionally were eminently pragmatic: editors would soon discover the facts. "We know we've got to live with these editors long after the client is gone."

There was an additional danger, someone else pointed out: an unethical client might frighten away ethical ones. Another participant had a succinct solution: "If you don't need the business, don't touch it. If you do need it, take a chance on it and go as far as you feel that you can without hurting yourself." But there was a further dimension to the ethical problem, Mrs. M. Luz of Ruder & Finn pointed out: the proprietors of a PR firm had an ethical responsibility to their employees and families. Was it right to prejudice their well-being by turning down clients because of abstract moral scruples? There ensued a long and inconclusive discussion about the connection between ethics and "economic status." If there was any concensus, it was that a certain "flexibility" had to be shown by the PR practitioner.

Another round table devoted itself to the problem of how to reconcile a client's private interest with the public interest. Paul Zucker, executive vice-president at R & F, outlined three situations which had sorely troubled R & F's collective conscience. In one case, the firm had done a spectacular job promoting a new tranquilizer, only to discover at the end of a year that the drug had harmful side effects. Was it R & F's responsibility to persuade the client that "we should do something about this"? Should it give up the account if the client refused?

Zucker was equally concerned about the propriety of promoting the sale of liquor. "Vodka does nothing for you, but a client pays us a fee to promote the sale of vodka." Was this ethical? More troublesome was a problem which had arisen in publicizing a new liquid form of aspirin. It was safer than tablet aspirin, which sometimes accidentally led to the poisoning of children. Would R & F be justified in trying to promote its client's product by hammering away at the potential dangers in the rival drug? Would the firm truly be serving the public interest or merely using "a pseudo-public-service approach to get our products sold?"

Again a concensus was difficult to attain. One view was that the PR man was blameless if he took the profitable way out. The fault lay with a business system dependent on all forms of salesmanship. Another participant would present the truth about the tranquilizer drug, come what may. A third suggested that it was "the reporter, the journalist . . . who has the luxury of speaking out the truth." Objectivity was necessarily denied the publicist. This was not a matter of great consequence, someone else suggested: "I think the public is attuned enough to public relations and advertising that a mild misrepresentation does not really do any serious damage." That was perhaps the most reassuring thought offered at the session.

The conference, one gathered, was a useful cathartic experience for the participants even if it did not lead to any ringing declarations of a brave new day in public relations. Reading over the proceedings, one has the impression that the bulk of the group regarded as suicidal any rigid adherence to the ethical canons whose propriety they would all formally acknowledge. Moreover, whenever an experienced PR man recommended an elevated course of conduct, it was usually on prudential grounds. None of this was as surprising as the apparent eagerness to assuage guilt through candid self-revelation.

The problem of client selection, honesty with the media and regard for the public interest hardly exhaust the ethical dilemmas of the PR man. A whole cluster of questions relate to the way he runs his own shop. In a great many PR accounts, the client is charged a fee and is billed separately for out-of-pocket expenditures. Is it proper to tack a commission on to those expenditures? Opinion is divided. Is it ethical to solicit clients? Many PR men (though usually only the most successful) insist that they hold themselves to the restraints imposed on lawyers or doctors. Others argue that they are in business and can with propriety act as aggressively as other businessmen.

There is somewhat greater agreement that it is bad form to steal another counselor's clients. Solicitation should be limited to companies which have no PR representation or which have indicated a desire to switch allegiance. This is a rule, however, which is often honored in the breach—blatantly by young and struggling firms and more discreetly by better established ones. The usual ploy is to use a friendly intermediary to sound out the prospect and invite a presentation. On the other hand, the rule that a PR firm does not represent competing clients is generally adhered to. The clients themselves insist on it.

None of these questions admit to easy answers. As Stephen Fitzgerald, a veteran PR consultant, has put it, "We are torn—

we are trying to act professionally and at the same time are troubled by how far we can go to get business. The reason we want to act professionally is that we don't want to become a bunch of cheap press agents. I would like to be decent and discreet and in good taste. Those are the guiding words."

How difficult they are to live by is indicated by some of PR's relationships with the media. There is general agreement that "outright bribery," as Ruder & Finn once put it, should not be condoned. But what constitutes bribing a journalist? Is it bribery, David Finn on one occasion asked, to hire an editor, with whom one normally tries to plant stories, to write a brochure for a client? Purists would perhaps detect a major conflict of interest, but Finn was not so sure.

Even outright bribery, while hardly widespread, is more prevalent than one might gather from the PR journals. In their more relaxed moments—and not for attribution—PR men will cite chapter and verse. It is not uncommon to be approached by an intermediary with the suggestion that a fifty-dollar bill will guarantee "picture placement" in a metropolitan daily. One practitioner tells of his surprise, when he was new to the field, to discover that a client regularly received a favorable play in a specialty column in a New York paper through the simple expedient of slipping a couple of hundred dollars to the columnist concerned whenever he exhibited his wares in New York. Sometimes the procedure was even more blatant. In one celebrated proxy fight, a publicity man representing one contestant merely walked into a newspaper city room and placed a release, with a hundred-dollar bill under it, on a financial writer's desk. In this case, the writer threw him out.

In the sports world, promoters have long regarded it as prudent to keep a few newspaper reporters on their payrolls—generally writers on boxing, wrestling and racing. Back in 1954, for example, the Providence *Journal-Bulletin* revealed that twenty-six newspapermen, employed by nine newspapers and two wire services, were listed by New England racing tracks as having received $30,000 in 1953. Rockingham Park in New Hampshire alone paid out $12,000 to eleven sports writers. The general manager of the track was quoted as saying that some writers were paid "for not doing a damn thing" and others assisted in the track's publicity department.

On occasion the practice of subsidizing sports writers is remarkably open. The story is told of an indignant boxing promoter who one day called on the publisher of a Midwest daily. The promoter complained that he was paying one of the paper's writers $150 a week and was not getting a fair shake in his column. The publisher, a newcomer to the newspaper business, promptly called in the errant writer and asked, "Is our friend here paying you $150 a week?" Taken aback, the sports writer sputtered that that was indeed the case.

"And what do you suppose he's paying you for?" the publisher inquired.

"To get a break," the sports writer admitted sheepishly.

"Then why the hell don't you give him one?" the publisher demanded.

In the great majority of newspaper shops, on the other hand, gratuities to sports writers are not tolerated; where they are, such outside income is used to justify low salaries.

Politicians in command of state funds have also been known at times to subsidize friendly journalists. In 1949, the St. Louis *Post-Dispatch* and the Chicago *Daily News* revealed that fifty-one publishers, editors and other employees were on the Illinois state payroll during the administration of Governor Dwight H.

Green from 1941 to 1949. They received a total of $480,000. Some of the newspapermen did work at state jobs, but the duties of many, according to the *Post-Dispatch,* were "to print canned editorials and news stories lauding the accomplishments of the Republican state administration." The exposé created a sensation in Illinois and led the American Society of Newspaper Editors to condemn both the former state administration and the complaisant newspapermen. Other journalists were later revealed to be on the public payroll in Florida, Georgia, and Albany, N.Y.

Relations with magazine writers are also a touchy subject. Practitioners regard it as ethical to pay a writer's expenses, if the magazine cannot afford to do so, while he is researching an article about a client. The point of propriety turns on the question of whether the magazine knows who is subsidizing the writer. It is the responsibility of the writer to tell, says the PR fraternity. The magazine might well feel that an inevitable conflict of interest is created, but many editors do not seem to mind.

The public relations departments of airlines frequently arrange for free transoceanic trips for writers, in exchange for plugs in their copy. Legally, the airlines cannot provide free transportation. The restriction is circumvented, however, by having the writer sign a contract whereby the airline pays him a certain sum in return for favorable mention in his articles. The writer then purchases his ticket from the airline. In some cases editors are aware of the practice, in others not. In all cases, what is involved is a certain debasement of the editorial columns.

While expense money is regarded as proper, there is general agreement in the PR field that a writer should not be paid a fee for an article for which he is also paid by a magazine. No PR outfit will openly concede that it does this, though the practice is not uncommon. A publicity break in a large magazine, with a circulation in the millions, can be worth a small fortune to a company making a consumer product. Overzealous PR men will sometimes offer as much as five thousand dollars to a writer if he can get the puff into print in the proper place. There are also more discreet ways of handling the matter—such as agreeing in advance to compensate the writer for a certain number of reprints or paying him a consultant's fee for undertaking some fictitious chore.

Where the magazine is unaware of the arrangement, which is usually the case, great embarrassment can occur if the editors inadvertently delete plugs for the PR client's product. Then the distressed writer is likely to plead that he owes an obligation to the publicity man, in return for co-operating on the research, to include some mention of his client. Rarely will the writer confess that he has been paid. He risks being barred from the magazine in the future.

Only a minority of journalists, on either newspapers or magazines, succumb to these dismaying practices; they assuredly bear as much responsibility as the PR men involved. Moreover, many publications show an amazing unconcern about the sources of the material they publish. The job of the PR firm may be to present its message in as innocuous a package as possible, but many editors hardly bestir themselves to see if there is a hidden gimmick or a controversy on which another side should be heard.

The same question of responsibility is involved in the issue of free trips and "loot." At Christmas time, and on other occasions around the year, PR men feel moved to dispatch tangible expressions of their esteem to friendly editors and reporters. These tokens can be as modest as a bottle of whiskey or a pair of theater tickets or as lavish as the thousand dollars in Tiffany trinkets which one press agent—a young lady of impeccable taste—bestowed on the staff of a leading television show after her employer had received especially handsome treatment. In its own defense, PR practitioners maintain that no bribery is involved; these are all gifts, bereft of strings. It is a dubious argument, but on the other hand some journalists regard such offerings as a normal perquisite of office. The PR man may be the seducer, but does the seduced share none of the blame?

14

The PR
Life

"In the old days," says a veteran PR hand, "aspiring writers and dramatists would get jobs on newspapers. Today they go into public relations." There is much truth to the observation. Small-town journals still need trained hands, but newspaper jobs in the big cities were obviously much easier to get in the period during World War I when there were 2,461 daily papers than in 1959 when there were 1,750. Public relations has more than taken up the slack. It is not only a refuge for aspiring writers, but is also the promised land for the bright crop of college youngsters who each year take the hundreds of courses in public relations which a 1956 survey indicated were being given by 136 colleges and universities. At Boston University, there is even a School of Public Relations and Communications.

I remember running into a young man in Westport, Connecticut who was about to be released from the army and was uncertain whether to essay journalism, advertising or public relations. He found the three fields equally appealing, but was rather struck with the "glamour" of public relations. It is not an unusual attitude among the untutored, though some veteran practitioners might dispute the term. Glamorous or not, there is a recognizable PR life. As previously mentioned, an employee of a corporate PR department is likely to lead a less frenetic existence than an executive in an independent consulting firm. The work of a government public relations man usually bears little similarity to that of an entertainment press agent. And yet there are certain categories of experience, satisfaction and frustration which are common to the field.

As with any occupational group, the mores of the successful represent the aspirations of the multitude. A Ben Sonnenberg can help set the tone of public relations even though there is little chance that competitors will imitate his extravagances. Not every PR man can afford to take prospective clients or hungry journalists to the shrines of the gastronomic arts which Sonnenberg frequents. Nonetheless, public relations' own public image is shaped by the folk customs and foibles of that energetic band of entrepreneurs whose main street is Madison Avenue and whose horizons stretch from Palm Springs to Cap Ferrat.

We are speaking here, of course, of the independent PR firm. The PR life in this setting is characterized by an insistent courtship of both client and journalist, in a manner either subtle or exuberant, depending on the personality of the PR man, but usually with appropriate gustatory or alcoholic accompaniment and such additional tokens of good fellowship as free theater tickets and boxed cigars in the hotel room. The most successful PR men will escort their charges to "21," Le Pavillon, the Chambord, the Colony and one or two other establishments where an ample lunch for two with a decent wine can hardly be had at a price under thirty dollars. PR men with shorter expense accounts will settle for the likes of Louis XIV or Toots Shor's, where the host can escape for fifteen dollars or less, depending on how much the guest drinks. Entertainment press agents prefer to be seen at Sardi's or the Algonquin. A private club often has greater éclat, though usually poorer food. But whatever the setting, the principle is the same: a discreet effort to put your quarry in your debt.

Some PR men recognize no distinction between their workday and their leisure hours, being cheerfully prepared to entertain a client around the clock, if need be. Sonnenberg's home, after all, is only a catering establishment in the guise of a residence. Such independent spirits as Dave Finn and Bill Ruder, on the other hand, maintain that they never entertain clients in the evening. This is highly eccentric behavior, however.

In a field as broad as public relations, there are of course many individuals, particularly on the staffs of corporations, who neither have to cultivate journalists nor court clients. These are specialists who may devote all their time to preparing annual reports, editing house organs, conducting research or guiding an educational-aids program. There are also full-time speech writers and pamphleteers who seldom emerge from their cubicles. All these people are in public relations, but they are hardly in the main stream. So long as they are confined to these pursuits, they are unlikely either to make spectacular salaries or achieve much responsibility. The basic public relations type is the salesman, though he appears in many guises and though he sells an impalpable commodity—the magic which can be performed by the written word and the visual image. To be successful, a PR man need not be able to sell both clients and journalists. But he must have an affinity for one or the other group. Indeed, in many PR shops there is a division of labor: one partner runs the publicity operation while the other soothes the distempers of clients and prospects for new accounts.

Much has been said in previous chapters of the variety of ways in which clients are attracted. Ben Sonnenberg's approach varies considerably from Earl Newsom's: they could no more exchange methods than swap haberdashery, yet each is successful. Retaining clients requires equal talent. As Paul Zucker, executive vice-president of Ruder & Finn, once put it: "A friend of mine with another public relations agency has said that the optimist uses the 'starting to work' time as a time for rejoicing, whereas the pessimist thinks 'now that we have them, when are we going to lose them?'"

There are many ways to lose clients. Overexuberant selling can raise expectations to unrealistic levels: no sooner is the contract signed than the client expects a platoon of *Life* photographers to descend on his plant. Ruder & Finn makes a habit of telling new accounts that it takes a year to break into the *Reader's Digest* (it often takes much longer, and requires an excellent story as well). Unsophisticated clients often have no notion of how much effort their PR man is expending on their behalf: when they finally emerge in the business section of *Time*, they may assume that merit won its own unaided reward. The solution, as any experienced PR man knows, is adequate "communication" with the client: give him a monthly report detailing every foray made in his behalf.

There is some dispute on how best to retain the loyalty of a new account. One school argues for immediate and dramatic results; another suggests that the ensuing months are likely to be anticlimactic, and the client may well become disillusioned. At a Ruder & Finn conference mentioned earlier, Herbert Kraus of Chicago regaled the assemblage with an hilarious account of how his firm solidified its relationship with an ice-cream manufacturer. Three months after starting work, Kraus sought a "gimmick" which would produce a great volume of publicity. Opportunity arrived in the form of the Soviet farm delegation, which was to visit Chicago on its tour of the Midwest. Vain efforts were made to get the Russians to visit the ice-cream plant, then one of Kraus's colleagues developed the bright idea of getting his client to manufacture five gallons of borscht ice cream and persuaded the Russians' hosts, an august foreign policy group, to allow the dessert to be presented at the dinner. Originally there was to be no publicity about the dinner, but Kraus was allowed to put out a story that the Russians were going to consume the rare ice cream. The newspapers, wire services, radio and television stations all played up the item. Kraus's client made the presentation, while the photographers snapped away. "Since then we have got no trouble with this client," Kraus reported. "Anything that we suggest, he likes. He never turns down anything and he takes our word."

Not every PR man is equally fortunate; some clients would expect to repeat the hoopla every second month. Even more troublesome is the client who engages a PR firm for corporate publicity, while his real motive is a "personal build-up" which he is too embarrassed to avow. If the PR man misinterprets the real intention, he is in great jeopardy.

Dave Finn has told the story of going to work for a large company and receiving all the standard disclaimers of the president's interest in personal publicity. His associates, however, informed R & F that the contrary was the case; Finn's people then proceeded to develop several projects in which the president was featured. But when R & F presented the program to the company's board of directors, there was great objection to a personal build-up for anybody. And so, Finn stated, "We had to rewrite the program for their benefit—but at the same time keep a secret program in our minds in which the president did occupy a central position . . . this is the prototype problem of the secret program and the open program."

The weirdest variation on the prototype was encountered in another Ruder & Finn case. After the contract was signed with a new client, one of the company's chief executives privately informed R & F that the president was dying of cancer and had but six months to live. The real purpose of the PR program, of which the president was quite unaware, was to bring him a final burst of recognition before his untimely end. "We were very moved," said Finn. "And we developed a program and succeeded in getting quite a lot of recognition." But after a year the president was still alive. The tale, a complete fabrication, had been passed along to every PR man which the company had employed.

Equally dismaying was the experience of another PR firm, which discovered after several weeks on a new account that their client had simultaneously retained two or three other agencies without informing anyone of the duplication in services. The motive was simple: if publicity was a good thing, the more press agents the better. In this case, the PR firm refused to indulge the client.

The hazards of client relations hardly detract from the appeal of PR. There are, of course, many reasons why people enter the field. Some ex-newspapermen have little choice. "How did I get into this business?" echoes Bill Doll. "I didn't pick it. I had the normal press agent's background. I got fired off the *Herald Tribune*—I was on the city side—and so the next day I was a press agent." In the depression, another newspaper job was not easy to get. Since then, the persistent merger of newspapers and the collapse of several general circulation magazines have forced many journalists into public relations who would have preferred their former pursuits.

Others, both veteran newspapermen and neophytes, have been attracted by the greater economic opportunities which public relations seemed to offer. "I switched to get more money, I'll be frank about it," says Bob Sullivan, who handles financial publicity in the Ed Gottlieb office. "After ten years in the newspaper business, I was making ninety-five dollars a week. That was the top Newspaper Guild scale at the time. You'll find that many PR guys would still be on newspapers if they felt they could afford it."

Available data is much too sketchy to allow for accurate comparisons between salaries in public relations and in newspaper and magazine work. A survey by the Public Relations Society of America of 268 of its members in 1955–56 provided some suggestive figures, however. Of its respondents (who comprised 12.8 per cent of its membership at the time and who worked in all fields of public relations), PRSA found that 19 per cent earned under $10,000; 14 per cent earned between $10,000 and $12,000; 17 per cent between $12,000 and $15,000; 29 per cent between $15,000 and $25,000; 17 per cent, $25,000 and over; 4 per cent did not answer the question. These figures indicate a considerably higher salary range than on newspapers. In 1959, there was doubtless not a newspaper in the country where 29 per cent of editorial employees earned between $15,000 and $25,000. Magazines tend to pay more than newspapers, of course, yet the same generalization would hold for most of them.

This assumption is certainly in accord with the view of most people who go into public relations from the media.

PR jobs and media jobs are not too far out of line on the lower echelons. There are also editorial executive positions on newspapers and magazines which pay as much as top public relations jobs. But PR boasts many more such jobs; in either a consulting firm or a corporate department, there is just a higher proportion of officers to troops than in a newspaper or wire service office of comparable size.

In the early days, the great majority of PR recruits came from journalism. In recent years, however, a growing number of new employees have entered the field directly from college or from collateral pursuits such as advertising or market research. They have no notion of abandoning a noble but penurious calling so that they can support their families in decent style; they are simply businessmen attracted by the buoyant opportunities which public relations offers.

The attractions of public relations go beyond salary at any particular level. Since the field is continually expanding, rapid advancement is a common experience. A young man who goes to work for a New York PR factory at $7,500 a year can reasonably expect, if he is capable, to double his salary in four or five years. More dramatic success stories are not unusual. In 1948, Ted Mecke, Jr., then in his mid-twenties, was earning $5,000 as managing editor of the Germantown, Pennsylvania *Courier*, a good-sized weekly paper. That same year he took a job, at $6,000, in the Philadelphia field office of Ford's public relations department. He did sufficiently well by June 1950 to be dispatched to Dearborn headquarters, where he was put to work as a reporter in the news department. By August 1957 he was running the entire public relations operation, under vice-president

Charles Moore, who supervises both PR and advertising. If Mecke was making less than $25,000 a year, he was being cheated.

Venturesome types are frankly captivated by the prospect of starting a business of their own. The *sine qua non* is one trusting client; almost no capital is needed. The standard procedure for the aspiring entrepreneur is to find employment in a successful PR firm, obtain some experience and work himself up to the job of account executive. If he is lucky, and not overly burdened by a sense of loyalty, he can perhaps detach his account from his employer and set up shop for himself—a maneuver which is easier in the case of a modest-sized firm than in a well-established house laden with prestige. Failing to steal a client, the alternative is often to seek outside prospects by offering bargain prices. The scramble can be desperate at this stage, but the future rewards make it worth while.

Not every PR man, of course, has the entrepreneurial itch; many prefer the security of the going concern. There are other compensations, of which the pleasures of an expense account should not be minimized. The expense account cannot be viewed as merely a material addition to the PR man's standard of living; it involves psychic gratifications which are perhaps more important. In a world where the cash nexus lies at the core of existence, an ability to distribute largesse produces a certain inflation of the personality. One asserts a measure of dominance, however transitory, by being able to play host two or three times a day.

When questioned, PR men prefer to dwell on the other satisfactions of their calling. They speak of the "variety" and "challenge" of the problems that confront them; the "longer time span" in public relations than in journalistic work, where there is nothing deader than yesterday's newspaper; and the "sense of participation" which they enjoy. The journalist is the outsider, continually prying into other people's affairs; the PR man, if he is fortunate, sits with the movers and shakers, helping to direct strategy.

A position near the fulcrum of power is often very appealing, whether the organization concerned is a corporation, a labor union or a government department. Even where there is no sharing in the exercise of power, there is an understandable satisfaction in being privy to inside information. Ted Mecke, for example, speaks with retrospective pleasure of one of his early assignments for the Ford Motor Company: preparing the "dry runs" of Ford's annual report, some years before the corporation became a public company and actually published the document. While the entire financial world speculated about Ford's balance sheet, young Mecke was among the few individuals who had access to the data. "Got quite a bang out of it," he says.

On a somewhat different level, Jay Scott recalls his relationship with Roy Fruehauf of the Fruehauf Trailer Company. Fruehauf was a client of Ben Sonnenberg's, and Scott used to work on the account. "When Roy was in town, we'd sit up until all hours at the Waldorf, discussing his most intimate business problems," Scott recalls. Such close communion with the mighty, one gathers, was not vouchsafed Scott when he was a mere newspaper reporter.

To many PR men, however, there are countervailing disadvantages to their way of life. When a firm loses one or two large accounts, there may be a flurry of staff dismissals. Then there is the daily necessity of being cast in the role of supplicants, continuously obliged to ask favors of the press. As one disillusioned practitioner put it, "Frankly, I'm weary of calling up people whom I've encountered in a different context and knowing, while we exchange amenities, that they're wondering whether I'll ask for something. And, by God, I never disappoint them! You become in a sense a second-class citizen, a beggar for small favors. An advertising executive, after all, is in a much better psychological position. He pays for space or time and then proceeds to fill it. But the PR man must always persuade someone —or bribe him—to get something in print. At times it can become humiliating."

The thick-skinned are apparently adjusted to rebuffs and the need for persistent entreaty. Yet the dismay which even the hardiest operators occasionally feel is revealed by the wistful envy with which they regard the upper echelon of PR counselors. "How I'd like to be Earl Newsom!" one veteran was heard to exclaim after three martinis. "In that job you don't have to be nice to anybody, you don't have to ask for special consideration —you're just paid to think." A slight exaggeration, no doubt; even Newsom has to be pleasant to his clients, but he is relieved of having to court the press. The same exemption, except in rare instances, is shared by the heads of most large agencies; they employ underlings for "press contact." But as one PR man put it, "The pay-off is always in the media. No matter how much counseling goes on, someone in the end must pick up a phone and ask a favor."

It is, of course, not always a painful process. If a publicity man has a good story, little exertion is required to break the papers. If an institution has "complete acceptance"—such as that enjoyed by, say, U. S. Steel or the Rockefeller family—a press agent can maintain the reserve of a banker and still have reporters pounding on his door. But most practitioners are not in this fortunate position.

Sensitive souls are also uncomfortable at the extent to which the PR man is compelled to convert friendship into a business asset. In public relations more than in other pursuits (politics excepted) every social relationship, sentimental association, old-school-tie connection is a prop in an endless game of self-aggrandizement. As a type, the PR man is the personification of what David Riesman called the "inside dopester." No inside dopester can function without sources, real or imagined; thus, the art of name-dropping is more than an amiable social gambit; it is a serious business tactic, designed to impress present and future clients with the PR man's easy familiarity with the potentates of industry and government. But name-dropping alone is not enough; the accomplished inside dopester must be in a position to pass along scraps of information which are not yet in the public domain. Everything is grist for his gossip mill—an anticipated stock split, a corporate shake-up, the casting of a new Broadway play, a new departure in foreign policy or in Parisian *haute couture*. Even in his idlest moments, sunning himself at Eden Roc or watching the races at Belmont, the inside dopester is feverishly at work. Devotees of the art derive great relish from it; others object to the exertion involved and to the necessary exploitation of every passing friendship. Perhaps they should not be in public relations.

A more serious complaint is seldom voiced, for it goes to the core of the PR life. That is the enormous expenditure of energy on tasks which are essentially trivial. The detached observer can only wonder how talented individuals can devote their working lives to publicizing Venetian blinds, cognac, millinery, or the corporate image of a ball-bearing manufacturer, to mention only a few of the campaigns cited in this volume. What are the professional (as opposed to the monetary) satisfactions of promoting a doughnut-making machine or a new-model Thunder-bird or even the higher economics as determined by the United States Steel Corporation?

The answer in large part depends on the background of the individual concerned. PR men who once nurtured serious aspirations as journalists often chafe under the inadequacy of their daily missions. To their intimates they justify their frustrations, if they refer to them at all, in terms of the collateral pleasures of the PR life. They may also try to derive satisfaction out of sheer technical virtuosity, regardless of the ends to which it is put. Or they may reflect that many journalistic jobs are dull and unrewarding. Yet the canker of discontent often remains.

PR men who lack journalistic background are unlikely to be troubled by this complaint. With no image of themselves as potential rivals to Lippmann or Alsop, they find public relations as congenial as merchandising or advertising. They see no need to justify their being in trade and can be indifferent, as most businessmen are, to the product they are pushing. If they are called upon to argue the point, which seldom happens, they would merely suggest that there is the same social utility in publicizing ball bearings as in manufacturing them.

These reflections, of course, are most relevant to employees of independent PR firms, whose clients may produce anything from cosmetics to sheet metal. Practitioners who are employed by corporations, labor unions, government bureaus or nonprofit groups often compensate for any dissatisfactions in their routine by identifying with their organization. John Sattler, who heads Ford's PR operation in New York, speaks in a disarming way of the prestige of representing so substantial an outfit as the Ford Motor Company. Frank Winn, who for years has headed the publicity setup of the United Automobile Workers, thinks of himself not so much as a PR technician as a votary of the labor movement. A government information officer regards himself as a civil servant rather than as a press agent whose services are available to any bidder. In the nonprofit field, the sense of participation in noble causes often compensates, as well, for relatively low salaries and limited perquisites.

The vaguest malaise of the PR practitioner is perhaps the most general: the sense of undefined status which afflicts the PR practitioner to an extent unknown to other specialists in the communications arts. There was a time when the advertising man felt compelled to defend his contribution to the consumer's well-being. However spurious the defense, it no longer seems necessary. Newspapermen (with the exception, of course, of "the gentleman from the *Times*" in the old joke) used to be regarded as uncouth interlopers. These days they are welcomed at diplomatic dinners. But the PR man, despite the vast budgets often at his command, is still looked upon with widespread skepticism. There is more suspicion than knowledge of just how he operates; his very reputation as a clever manipulator tends to frustrate his continual striving for professional recognition. It is a sorry frustration, which accounts for much of the solemn rhetoric about the "mission" of public relations and for the small sputter of celebration every time another colleague ascends the corporate ladder to vice-president.

15

And
the Results?

For some years now public relations activities have been an accepted part of the folkways of American life. Many PR practitioners have made fortunes. A huge literature, much of it ponderous and self-serving, has sprung up to celebrate the achievements of the new calling. A variety of extravagant claims have been advanced in its behalf. Indeed, one practitioner has even stated: "To public relations men may go the most important social engineering role of them all: the gradual reorganization of human society, piece by piece and structure by structure."

Confronted with all the rhetoric, the uncommitted observer can fairly ask exactly what public relations can prove it accomplishes. It depends, of course, on what one means by proof. Precise validation, by means of elaborate before-and-after opinion testing, with due allowance for all the variables which affect attitude formation, is extremely difficult to come by. On the other hand, an impressionistic assessment of the various scraps of evidence which bob up in the wake of a PR campaign is relatively easy and commonplace. At times an informed judgment can be made on the basis of scattered evidence; at other times the judgment represents pure wish fulfillment and the understandable desire of the PR man to retain the account. The client often has an equal interest in affirming success: he may hate to admit that his enthusiasm for public relations has been misplaced.

The problem of testing the impact of a PR campaign is an old one for social scientists who specialize in opinion research: how to gauge the degree to which the mass media influence opinion, taste, conduct? A host of studies on this subject over the past two decades have come to contradictory conclusions. In some instances, the media were found to have no significant persuasive effect; in others—such as efforts to sell war bonds— they were shown to be very effective indeed.

The problem, basically, is that in many situations the impact of mass communications is diluted by various factors. As Joseph T. Klapper put it in a perceptive address in 1957, "What We Know About the Effects of Mass Communication: The Brink of Hope," which later appeared in the *Public Opinion Quarterly*, Vol. 21, No. 4: "The relatively placid waters of 'who says what to whom' were early seen to be muddied by audience predispositions, 'self-selection,' and selective perception. More recent studies, both in the laboratory and the social world, have documented the influence of a host of other variables . . . the audiences' image of the source; the simple passage of time; the group orientation of the audience member and the degree to which he values group membership; the activity of opinion leaders; the social aspects of the situation during and after exposure to the media . . . his social class, and the level of his frustration . . ."

The findings of the social scientists, in this as in many matters, confirm everyday observation. (This is no criticism; validation of clichés is useful, for they are often untrue.) Thus, in an election campaign one has observed how impervious a confirmed Democrat or Republican can be to the propaganda of the other side; deeply held convictions are hard to shake. In the Eisenhower years, on the other hand, urban Democrats, after they moved to the suburbs, frequently began to vote as their Republican neighbors did; a shift in environment can obviously change attitudes—and often more significantly than what is read or seen on television. In strikes, the newspapers may be filled with hostile polemics, and yet the strikers' resistance is unimpaired; group loyalty is a very strong thing.

With so many factors bearing on opinion formation and inhibiting shifts in opinion, it is naturally difficult to isolate and measure the impact of what is communicated by the mass media. Klapper, however, thinks it is possible if one uses a "phenomenistic approach." He favors "a shift away from the tendency to regard mass communication as a necessary and sufficient cause of audience effects, toward a view of the media as influences, working amid other influences, in a total situation. The old quest of specific effects stemming directly from the communication has given way to the observation of existing conditions or changes—followed by an inquiry into the factors, including mass communication, which produced those conditions and changes . . ." More often than not, according to the "emerging generalizations" which Klapper goes on to formulate, the media are likely to reinforce rather than change existing attitudes. Where change does occur, he suggests, it is in situations where the influences apart from communication are inoperative or are

themselves tending toward change. He leaves an out, however
—"residual situations in which mass communication seems to
wreak direct effects . . ."

Klapper regards his generalizations as propelling us toward
"the brink of hope" that the influence of the mass media can be
adequately gauged. This may well be the case; but his formula-
tion of the problem also indicates the enormous difficulty of
measuring the effectiveness of a public relations effort of any
complexity.

It is hardly enough to know the existing state of affairs, to
observe a change, and to assume that the intervening PR campaign produced the change. We have already dealt at length
with the Hill and Knowlton campaign in behalf of the natural
gas producers. The desired legislation ultimately passed the
Congress, but not even Hill and Knowlton claims credit for the
success. Several things would have had to be measured: the impact of the PR campaign on opinion around the country (either
in changing views, or activating latent support, or even activating latent opposition); the impact of such a mobilization of
opinion on members of Congress, as well as the direct impact
of the PR arguments on congressmen; the effectiveness of the
concurrent lobbying campaign; the internal politics of each
chamber at the time, which might well have affected voting regardless of the arguments and pressures on either side on this
particular issue; and doubtless other factors as well. It would
hardly be beyond the ingenuity of our social scientists to devise
a study which would weigh all these circumstances, but it would
be a cumbersome and an expensive business.

Even in a simple product publicity campaign, results are not
easy to measure with any precision. Ed Gottlieb is hired to boost
cognac; sales go up, but advertising appropriations go up *pari*

passu; how much of the sales increase is due to advertising, how much to greater effort on the part of salesmen, how much to PR? Moreover, what percentage increase, if any, is due to greater consumption of liquor generally? How much of the increase, if any, is due neither to PR nor to media advertising but to word-of-mouth advertising or to increased travel in Europe with the subsequent development of new acquired tastes? Similar questions can be asked in every product publicity campaign.

Another area of PR—the counseling function—can hardly be measured even if one should want to. Public relations men at times liken their role to that of doctors practicing preventive medicine. But it is impossible to be certain about the effectiveness of prophylaxis—except with masses of people. How can one determine that the patient would otherwise have contracted the disease? In a choice between alternate courses of corporate action, one knows, after the fact, the consequences of Course A, but can never be certain what would have been the consequences of Course B, against which the PR man counseled. Suppose one provoked a strike rather than prevented one; "spun off" a subsidiary rather than retained it; propitiated a business rival rather than fought him—who can measure "scientifically" the alternate consequences?

Some companies do make an effort to assess their standing with the public, with a view to gaining some insight into what affected public attitudes. Since 1937, a number of leading corporations have subscribed to a service of The Psychological Corporation called the Audit of Company Reputation (formerly the Link Audit). Through interviews around the country, the Audit seeks to determine "How well acquainted American adults are with your company, as compared with ninety-nine other leading companies in over twenty different industries, and how favorably people acquainted with your company regard it, relative to these other companies." Details are also offered concerning the sorts of people who know the company, what they know about it, how they evaluate products and services and so on. Comparisons from year to year in a company's reputation are also provided.

All this is doubtless of considerable interest to a corporation, but it does not provide much of a guide to the effectiveness of a public relations program. One can trace the fluctuations in corporate reputation, but it is difficult to pinpoint the causes—unless they represent major departures. Thus, as Phelps Adams, U. S. Steel PR director points out, when there is a strike, his company's reputation drops appreciably, to recover after the strike is over. (This is a common experience for many companies.) On the Audit's graph, he can also point to a marked upswing in favorable opinion in 1950 when the company head, Benjamin Fairless, started to make speeches; there was a similar affirmative response a few years later when U. S. Steel launched its television program. But a detailed evaluation of the effectiveness of U. S. Steel's public relations program is hardly provided by the Audit.

Another interesting assessment of corporate reputation was prepared by the Opinion Research Corporation in its 1958 study, "The Corporate Image." On the basis of interviews, it compiled "image profiles" of twenty-two large corporations—providing a wealth of detail as to the public's impressions of the company's products, advertising, quality of radio or television program, interest in research, contribution to the economy, support of education and a variety of other matters, on each of which percentage points of favorable or unfavorable response were listed. To provide comparisons over a span of time, Opinion

Research plans to resurvey the profiles at intervals in the future. As with The Psychological Corporation's Audit, this survey seems useful as an index to reputation, but of no great help in indicating what factors influenced the public's impressions.

A fair amount of testing is done of the individual tools of a public relations program—an employee publication, a literature rack in a factory, an annual report, a brochure written for the general public. The technique is to get people to read the material and then "play back" what they have gleaned from it. The Opinion Research Corporation has undertaken a number of such studies for its subscribers. Some years ago, for example, four pamphlets arguing the case against the excess profits tax were distributed among a group of rank-and-file citizens and then tested for audience reaction. A number of findings emerged as to which techniques had greater impact and caused a shift in opinion (cartoons were more effective than graphs, the plight of small companies won more sympathy than that of large companies), but there was no indication as to how lasting the persuasion was or what would happen if the same individuals were exposed to counterpropaganda. Nonetheless, this sort of research is of some utility.

Rarely is an attempt made, because of the complexities and expense involved, to test the impact of an entire PR program. One of the few such efforts was undertaken by the American Cancer Society, which in 1948 and again in 1955 conducted national surveys "of public reaction to cancer." The results indicated, among other things, that after seven years 59 per cent rather than 51 per cent of the sample could name "the seven danger signals of cancer," that there was "some reduction in the percentage subscribing to erroneous beliefs . . . about cancer," that 60 per cent of the knowledgeable group as compared to

31 per cent previously had obtained their information from the mass media, and that more than 75 per cent, as compared to 51 per cent in 1948, identified the Cancer Society as the organization raising funds to combat cancer. Inasmuch as the ACS was the principal source of propaganda about cancer—appealing directly to the public as well as stimulating the media—these results could be taken as indicating a measure of success. Studies of national attitudes on most issues, however, would hardly lead to so neat a conclusion, for there would normally be many fonts of information and propaganda on any issue.

In truth, public relations men are not overly eager that clients test their programs by polling techniques: the results are too unpredictable. A few years ago, for example, The Psychological Corporation tested a PR campaign in northern California for a large manufacturer. Some two thousand interviews were employed, a thousand before the program was launched and a thousand afterwards. The PR campaign was very intensive, employing all media to increase familiarity with the product and to suggest the importance of the company to the economy of the area. When the results were in, the company found virtually no change in the "before" and "after" responses. The PR effort had had no discernible effect.

From the point of view of the public relations man, validating a program in an impressionistic way is of course a safer technique—and is not always without merit. The ease with which a program can be appraised by informal methods is in direct ratio to the narrowness of the target. Press agentry in the entertainment world, to take one extreme, has reasonably limited goals: to puff the reputation of a performer or to push the sale of tickets. If attendance at a theater increases after a clever stunt, and if there has been no increase in advertising during the same period, the press agent can reasonably claim credit.

In the corporate field, the PR man is on equally sound ground when he is pushing a product. An article about a consumer item in a leading national magazine has demonstrable selling power: a flood of new orders often follows immediately. Similarly, $100,000 devoted to a year's PR campaign to promote thumbtacks or ballpoint pens can be considered worth while or not when the sales figures come in. The method may be unprecise, but one can often make an informed guess as to how much credit should be apportioned to the advertising program, to the increased effort of salesmen, and to public relations.

Indeed, so valuable is product publicity in magazines and newspapers that one PR outfit—the Medical Research Association—is able to charge clients a staggering fee for each major news break. As its name indicates, MRA specializes in researching and publicizing the medical claims of consumer products. Smirnoff Vodka and a reducing candy known as Ayds have been among its accounts. In one presentation to a prospective client, MRA asked the following scale of fees: $25,000 to conduct the initial research; $10,000 for the reading of a medical paper on its results; $25,000 for a single news break in either AP, UPI or Science Service; and, on a sliding scale, depending on the magazine, $15,000 to $50,000 for a single placement in a magazine.

Product publicity is not, of course, the only area where the achievements of public relations are relatively easy to measure. The same can be said for specific short-run campaigns—to defeat a piece of legislation, to pass a referendum measure, to win a proxy fight. In a California referendum contest, where each side is represented by a PR firm, the winning side can reasonably attribute a good deal of the credit to its campaign managers.

Not all the credit, of course, for many influences may have entered into the outcome; an accurate apportionment of responsibility would indeed require elaborate studies by the opinion-samplers.

Limited objectives, especially in areas where few people are agitated one way or the other, are especially susceptible to public relations campaigning. "It was reasonably easy," says Hill and Knowlton's Bert Goss, "to oppose successfully a bill to have the government take over the fertilizer plants or a proposal to have the government build steel mills. They were easy to lick because the public couldn't care less." But when a campaign has broader objectives—to create a favorable impression on the public at large, to win a reputation for corporate innovation or dedication to the public interest—one enters an area where impressionistic measurement is undependable and where the effectiveness of a PR effort is always open to doubt.

Widespread and deeply held public attitudes, as has been suggested earlier, are not readily responsive to the persuasive techniques of public relations. Standard Oil (N.J.) has for years operated one of the most impressive public relations programs in the country; yet the company has never fully recovered from the attack by Ida Tarbell, more than half a century ago, on the parent Standard Oil trust, which has long since been broken up. "The Tarbell book," says Earl Newsom, "fixed a position for decades; it made the oil industry and anything connected with the oil industry a sitting duck for criticism."

Newsom is fond of referring to "The Cincinnati Experiment" of 1947 as an excellent example of the limitations of PR. For six months an extraordinary effort was expended to make Cincinnati "United Nations conscious." Mountains of literature were distributed, hundreds of meetings were held, the radio stations and the schools enthusiastically supported the program.

When it was over, writes Newsom, "only half as many people considered United Nations a means of preventing war as thought so at the beginning. There was almost no change in the number who thought the United States should take an active part in world affairs. At the beginning of the campaign, 76 per cent of Cincinnatians were in favor of having the United States join in the movement to set up an international police force to keep world peace. Six months later, 73 per cent felt that way."

Why the failure of the campaign? The reason, apparently, is that most people were supremely indifferent to the UN. It was remote from their lives, a disembodied concept. Moreover, as Newsom points out: ". . . the *actions* of the United Nations were weakening the confidence of people at the time the information program was in progress. Words were not so eloquent as actions. Under those conditions calling attention to the United Nations tended to 'unsell' rather than to 'sell.'" It is a problem from which many public relations programs have suffered.

Oftentimes, the question of effectiveness is sheer irrelevance; what is important is not what the PR practitioner does for the client, but what the client *thinks* he does. And there are a variety of ways to impress a client. The simplest is to overwhelm him with the fruits of publicity—clippings. Elaborate scrapbooks filled with clippings can be presented as a prima facie token of success, regardless of whether the splurge of publicity achieved the goals of increased sales or a shift in public attitude. Some firms go to elaborate lengths to dramatize their publicity breaks; among the gimmicks are plastering the walls at a trade convention with thousands of clips, or stuffing them into burlap bags and offering a prize for the closest estimate of their number. This looks impressive, but is really not very difficult to do; a large account may bring in four thousand clippings a month (including, of course, the multiple appearances of wire-service stories).

Measuring the effectiveness of publicity may also be irrelevant because, as observed in an earlier chapter, in some instances the real as opposed to the ostensible goal of a PR campaign is to feed the ego of the company president. What matter if the resultant publicity has little or no effect on sales figures or the luster of the corporate image so long as the president turns up, in one fashion or another, in the pages of *Time*, the New York *Times*, *Fortune*, the *Wall Street Journal* and perhaps even *The New Yorker?* Confronted with a client seeking a sunburst of recognition, the shrewd practitioner has only to keep the cameras trained on him to retain the account.

David Finn, in a speech on "The Social Consequences of Public Relations," has provided an interesting discussion of the effects of the standard PR technique of winning the support of "third parties"—organizations or individuals with presumably no financial stake in the matter at hand—in order to enhance the stature of a product or a company and thereby attract increased public support. The declared goal is always public approval, but so relentless is the pursuit of such "objectivity symbols" that they can become goals in themselves.

"In a sense," Finn writes, "the symbols are taken as a reflection of reality, and endorsement by these symbols has come to be another form of gratification by which the needs of the decisionmaker for social approval can be satisfied. . . . This trend may, actually, be a natural outgrowth of a materially successful society, in which prime movers no longer find the things that money can buy a sufficiently compelling motive for their ambitions." They yearn for the approval of the savants, the appearance of the governor at a ground-breaking ceremony, the bestowal of awards and the amassment of honors. It is a kind of gratification which public relations is peculiarly suited to furnish.

The client may be equally well impressed by a dexterous mobilization of the elaborate jargon of public relations, especially when it is coupled with shrewd insight into his psychological needs. An executive of a large corporation which retains one of New York's leading PR counselors has described the process by which his president's loyalty has been retained. The chief of the PR firm accompanies his account executive to each monthly meeting with the client. The PR man "has a positive genius for divining our boy's insecurities and playing up to them. The insecurities relate to his feeling, however unconscious, that he is really 'a robber' and also to his unfamiliarity with the great outside world of culture, politics, and so on. The PR guy is always able to persuade 'X' of his social stature, the importance of the company's 'mission,' he talks endlessly about the company's 'internal image' and 'external image.' He also name-drops like mad—'just saw Dick last night—Dick Nixon, you know.' That sort of thing. It works magnificently."

Whatever the success of PR in achieving specific goals, the character of its influence on American life is not difficult to perceive. It is a commonplace among social critics to deplore the whole institution. At its worst, public relations is regarded as an instrument of fraud and at its best as an unnecessary hindrance to communication.

Such wholesale condemnation is bootless as well as unfair. The public relations business, as its votaries continually suggest, is an inevitable outgrowth of a complex society. When the republic was young, face-to-face communication between buyer and seller, employer and employee, the church and its flock was relatively easy. Today the machinery of communications is so cumbersome that an intricate set of tools must be employed if an institution is to make effective contact with its "publics." Such is the rationale; there is a good deal of truth in it.

Much of public relations, of course, is salutory. No argument is needed on behalf of the "reporting function"—the straightforward dissemination of facts about government programs, industrial innovation, scientific discoveries or union plans. (Problems arise, of course, when the dissemination is not straightforward.) Every reporter appreciates the PR man who opens doors; few would care to see a return of the secrecy which characterized American industry around 1900.

However self-serving the motives, public relations has also been responsible for many good works on the part of business. The hospital and the foundation provide their own justification, even if their establishment was part of an elaborate effort to whitewash an errant corporation. The rhetoric of public service, though it is often cloying, does reflect a generally better relationship between industry and the community than that which prevailed fifty years ago. Public relations must receive at least some of the credit for awakening an enlightened self-interest.

The debit side, however, is equally impressive—and perhaps longer. Among its other derelictions, as previously noted, is the corrupting influence which PR sometimes has on the media. "Buying editors"—whether by a junket, Christmas "loot," a consultant's fee or outright bribery—is a trade custom denounced by moralists but invoked too frequently not to cause dismay. Morality aside, its effect is certainly to create a conflict of interest which hinders a newspaper or magazine in its proper function.

Corruption, however, is not the major problem. The more serious charge is that too often public relations tends not to further a free flow of information but to inhibit it—by promoting half truths in the guise of truths, by creating distractions, by invoking false authority, by simple deceit and by all manner of clever sleight of hand. The faked research project, the "kept" expert, the dubious medical claim, the subsidized "front" organization, the diversionary "created event" are among the techniques of public relations which manipulate rather than enlighten opinion. This is the major indictment: that public relations takes unfair advantage of an unsuspecting public.

And the indictment in many instances is accurate. Manipulation, as previously argued, is a complex matter. One might construct a scale of manipulative method. At one end, perhaps, would be rational argument flavored with emotional imagery likely to elicit a favorable response; at the other extreme would be a cluster of front groups and "objectivity symbols" set in motion for purposes of pure deception. The shadings in-between would be determined by the extent to which straightforward persuasion is replaced by the techniques of distortion.

Some PR campaigns, in other words, are more antisocial than others. Some are innocuous. The test to apply, of course, is not merely the relative degree of manipulation but also the purpose of the campaign. A stunt by a Broadway press agent can be highly manipulative, yet no one is moved to moral outrage. Manipulation in behalf of product promotion can often be laughed off, unless the manipulation is extreme or the product useless—or harmful. But when the machinery of deceit is employed in behalf of a significant social issue, a political campaign, a noxious foreign government or any other matter of substance, there can be ground for alarm.

Fortunately, however, there seems no present danger that the republic will be taken over by the public relations men, however vaulting their rhetoric. Our greatest safeguard against the professional manipulators is doubtless the vast reservoir of indifference, the enormous resistance to changing fixed opinions, which always characterizes the mass of people except in moments of crisis. A new breakfast food or a new form of aspirin can be easily merchandised, but public opinion on the great issues of the day is not readily maneuvered by a PR man in the clouds over Madison Avenue who throws a few switches and even dumps a few million dollars into the channels of communication. This is not to deny that significant victories may be scored by the side which moves most rapidly to mobilize latent support and even win over a few waverers from the opposition. Limited targets can indeed be attained by PR techniques. But in a democracy no one has a monopoly on persuasion, hidden or overt. There is usually a later opportunity to redress the balance. Even the advantage the business community possesses in the greater sums it allocates for propaganda is in good part balanced by the vast membership of the labor movement and its many internal paths of communication. And labor is not exactly penniless either.

There is no need to rely solely, however, on the automatic countervailing forces which public relations sets in motion. Certain reforms would be useful. Newspapers and magazines could clear the atmosphere considerably by adopting a few self-denying ordinances involving the largesse of the PR man—except for such trivia as luncheon invitations, which can easily be reciprocated. Even more helpful would be reporting of the public relations activity behind every significant news story. All too often, journalists seem to operate under an implicit compact to keep the PR man offstage and let his principal seem in full command of the situation. Perhaps because of the tradition of deadpan reporting of surface facts, the public relations implication of "created events," corporation strategy or government pronouncements (except in diplomatic exchanges) is seldom explored.

A front-page story in the New York *Times* of April 7, 1959, by Joseph A. Loftus, is a good example of the sort of news treatment which would have a healthy effect all around. The story was about a White House announcement on April 6 that unemployment figures, to be made public the following day, would show a substantial decline for the month of March. There was an obvious question as to why a preliminary announcement was made and why the news came from the White House rather than from the Commerce and Labor Departments. Most papers overlooked these matters. Loftus, however, informed his readers that the White House setting was a "departure from routine" and also noted that "The Administration was evidently making the most of the good business news in the best public relations fashion. There was no explanation of why the actual figures on unemployment would not be given out until tomorrow. The effect, however, is to spread the news accounts over two days instead of one."

We would all gain, in sum, if the PR man were edged out of the shadows and subjected to the glare of attention normally reserved for his clients. These days he is important enough to warrant continual scrutiny.

Index